Boston Red Sox Baseball

By The Numbers

Boston Red Sox Baseball

By The Numbers

Researched by Paul F. Wilson

Paul F. Wilson & Tom P. Rippey III, Editors

Kick The Ball, Ltd
Lewis Center, Ohio

By The Numbers Books by Kick The Ball, Ltd

College Football

Ohio State
Buckeyes

Pro Baseball

Boston   New York
Red Sox   Yankees

Visit us online at www.ByTheNumberBook.com

This book is dedictated to my new friends in New England, Lisa Ward, Bill McCann, Tom Robb, Anthony Schena, Rob Crocker and Kevin Barry

Boston Red Sox Baseball: By The Numbers;
First Edition 2011

Published by
Kick The Ball, Ltd
8595 Columbus Pike, Suite 197
Lewis Center, OH 43035
www.ByTheNumberBook.com

Edited by: Paul F. Wilson & Tom P. Rippey III
Copy Edited by: Ashley Thomas Memory
Designed and Formatted by Paul F. Wilson
Researched by: Paul F. Wilson

Copyright © 2011 by Kick The Ball, Ltd, Lewis Center, Ohio

ALL RIGHTS RESERVED. No part of this book may be reproduced or transmitted in any form whatsoever, electronic, or mechanical, including photocopying, recording, or by any informational storage or retrieval system without the expressed written, dated and signed permission from the copyright holder.

Trademarks and Copyrights: Kick The Ball, Ltd is not associated with any event, team, conference, or league mentioned in this book. All trademarks are the property of their respective owners. Kick The Ball, Ltd respects and honors the copyrights and trademarks of others. We use event, team, conference, or league names only as points of reference in our books. Names, statistics, and others facts obtained through public domain resources.

LIMIT OF LIABILITY/DISCLAIMER OF WARRANTY: THE RESEARCHER AND PUBLISHER HAVE USED GREAT CARE IN RESEARCHING AND WRITING THIS BOOK. HOWEVER, WE MAKE NO REPRESENTATION OR WARRANTIES AS TO THE COMPLETENESS OF ITS CONTENTS OR THEIR ACCURACY AND WE SPECIFICALLY DISCLAIM ANY IMPLIED WARRANTIES OF MERCHANTABILITY OR FITNESS FOR A PARTICULAR PURPOSE. WARRANTIES MAY NOT BE CREATED OR EXTENDED BY ANY SALES MATERIALS OR SALESPERSON OF THIS BOOK. NEITHER THE RESEARCHER NOR THE PUBLISHER SHALL BE LIABLE FOR ANY LOSS OF PROFIT OR ANY OTHER COMMERCIAL DAMAGES, INCLUDING BUT NOT LIMITED TO SPECIAL, INCIDENTAL, CONSEQUENTIAL, OR OTHER DAMAGES.

For information on ordering this book in bulk at reduced prices, please email us at pfwilson@bythenumberbook.com.

International Standard Book Number: 978-1-934372-94-4

Printed and Bound in the United States of America

10 9 8 7 6 5 4 3 2 1

Table of Contents

Numbers 1-25.. Page 1

Numbers 26-50... Page 26

Numbers 51-75...Page 51

Numbers 76-100... Page 76

About Kick The Ball, Ltd *By The Numbers* Books

"By The Numbers" books, articles, magazine features, etc. come in many formats. Most are done in pure chronological order, some match numbers in logical strings or related natural progressions within a category, and still others follow no easily discernable pattern at all.

As you turn the pages of this book, you will notice that we have categorized the numbers based on either the **final or final two digits** of each number. For example, you would find the year 1901 on page 1. The year 1910 would therefore be found on page 10, and so on.

In researching and compiling this book we found that to maintain our desired structure of a 1-100 grouping, this methodology would be necessary. Categorizing numbers 1-100 allows the reader to more quickly reference any given number based on the last digit or two, and gives us the ability to organize the data in exactly 100 pages.

This book is not meant to be exhaustive. Each researcher is given latitude to include a limited number of items they feel are particular important or interesting for each number. Additionally, other supportive or background numbers may be included with the primary number being presented. We do this to add depth to the information you are presented.

You will also notice **Featured Figure** sections spread throughout the pages of this book. These special sections include random, but interesting, information on a number relating to a particular moment or performance in team history.

All information in this book is valid as of the end of the 2010 season.

Boston Red Sox

BASEBALL

The Boston Red Sox, then known as the Boston Americans, played their first-ever game at the Baltimore Orioles, currently known as the New York Yankees, on April 26, 1901. Boston lost the game by four runs, 6-10.

The first World Series ever played was in 1903. The Boston Americans defeated the Pittsburgh Pirates 5-3 to win the league's inaugural and the team's first World Series.

Jimmy Collins was Boston's first manager. He was the team's skipper from 1901 through 1906, posting a 455-376 record for a .548 winning percentage.

The first year that Red Sox players wore numbers on their jerseys was 1931.

27,000 fans packed Fenway Park on April 20, 1912, to watch the first regular-season ball game ever played in the ballpark. Boston defeated the New York Highlanders 7-6 in 11 innings of play.

Cy Young pitched the American League's first-ever perfect game on May 5, 1904. His effort gave Boston a 3-0 victory over Philadelphia.

Bill Sweeney was the first Red Sox player to ever wear jersey No. 1. The number has not been worn since 1988 when it was retired by the Red Sox to honor Bobby Doerr.

By The Numbers

Boston Red Sox

BASEBALL

Two Red Sox have recorded unassisted triple plays. George Burns did it on Sept. 14, 1923, versus the Cleveland Indians and John Valentin accomplished this rare feat on July 8, 1994, versus the Seattle Mariners. So rare is the unassisted triple play that in the modern era only 15 of them have been recorded league wide.

Manny Ramirez and Mike Lowell are the only two Red Sox to be named World Series MVP. Manny earned the award in 2004 and Mike in 2007.

There are only two Red Sox with greater than 250 career stolen bases. Harry Hooper had 300 steals in 1,647 games from 1909-20. Tris Speaker had 267 in 1,065 games from 1907-15.

On Sept. 15, 1979, Bob Watson became only the second Red Sox to hit for the natural cycle. Leon Culberson was the first on July 3, 1943.

Only eight American Leaguers have ever won the batting Triple Crown. Two of them played for the Boston Red Sox. Ted Williams won it twice, once in 1942 and again in 1947, and Carl Yastrzemski in 1967.

Boston boasts two pitching Triple Crown winners, Cy Young in 1901 and Pedro Martinez in 1999.

Red Sox legend Cy Young had a 2.00 career ERA. He is ranked 2nd on the club's all-time leaders list for the category.

By The Numbers

Boston Red Sox

○ ○ ○ • • •

B
A
S

Boston has played host to three Major League Baseball All-Star Games at Fenway Park. In 1946, the American League defeated the National League in a 12-0 route; in 1961 they played to a tie, and in 1999 the American League won 4-1.

E
B
A

The Red Sox have won 100 or greater games in a season three times. The 1912 BoSox went 105-47, the 1915 team went 101-50 and the 1946 team had a 104-50 record.

L
L

The BoSox are the only team in Major League Baseball history to overcome a 0-3 deficit in the postseason to win a series. In 2004's ALCS the Red Sox engineered the historic three-game comeback versus the New York Yankees to earn their first trip to the World Series since 1918.

Three World Series games have ended in a tie. One of them took place in the 1912 World Series matchup between the Red Sox and New York Giants. With six runs each, Game 2 was called due to darkness after 11 innings. The Red Sox won the eight-game series, 4-3-1.

The Red Sox have never won fewer than three games in any of their Fall Classic appearances. The team has played in 11 World Series, winning seven of them and forcing a seventh game in each of their four losses.

The BoSox club record for the most consecutive years with a postseason appearance is 3 (2003-05 and 2007-09).

By The Numbers

Boston Red Sox

BASEBALL

Four charter members of the American League in 1901 continue to play ball in their original cities. The Boston Red Sox, Chicago White Sox, Cleveland Indians and Detroit Tigers have all survived 110 years of major league play in their respective cities.

Red Sox catcher Jason Varitek has caught four no-hitters, a record for MLB. Varitek caught no-hitters thrown by Hideo Nomo, Derek Lowe, Clay Buchholz and Jon Lester.

No Red Sox batter has ever hit four home runs in a single game. The opportunity has presented itself 25 times in club history, but no hitter has been able to top three.

What does it feel like to witness your team hit back-to-back-to-back-to-back home runs in an inning? Red Sox nation experienced that joy on April 22, 2007, when Manny Ramirez, J.D. Drew, Mike Lowell and Jason Varitek homered consecutively to rally back from a 0-3 deficit to the New York Yankees. Boston went on to win that game 7-6. Four consecutive home runs by a single team have happened only seven times in league history.

Jim Tabor (1939), Rudy York (1946), Nomar Garciaparra (1999) and Bill Mueller (2003) have each hit two grand slams in a single game. No other MLB team can boast having four players who hit two grand slams in a game.

By The Numbers

Boston Red Sox

ooo••• 5

BASEBALL

Journeyman Dave Roberts recorded five stolen bases for the Red Sox in the 2004 regular season, hardly a spectacular feat. And yet his only stolen base of the postseason that year may be the biggest stolen base in Boston Red Sox history. The stolen base in Game 4 of the ALCS sparked Boston's unprecedented rally against the Yankees and their eventual return to the World Series.

No big leaguer wants credit for a platinum sombrero, which is five strikeouts in a single game. Unfortunately Boston's Ray Jarvis and Phil Plantier both had it happen to them in a nine-inning contest. Jarvis struck out five times versus Cleveland on April 20, 1969. Plantier earned his platinum sombrero on Oct. 1, 1991, versus Detroit.

Following the Red Sox sweep of the St. Louis Cardinals in the 2004 World Series, an estimated 3 million-plus fans attended their victory parade on Oct. 30, 2004. That is nearly five times the population of Boston.

Five days following the sinking of the Titanic, the first-ever pro baseball game was played at Fenway Park. What would have been front-page news in Boston was obscured by the tragedy at sea that took the lives of 1,517 people on the morning of April 15, 1912.

Featured Figure

Cy Young pitched 275 complete games for Boston from 1901-08. No BoSox pitcher has ever pitched more complete games.

By The Numbers

•••ooo

Boston Red Sox

○ ○ ○ • • • ─────────────── 6

B
A
S
E
B
A
L
L

Six Red Sox pitchers have received the American League Cy Young award. Jim Lonborg was honored in 1967, Roger Clemens in 1986, 1987 and 1991, and Pedro Martinez in 1999 and 2000.

In 2007, Dustin Pedroia became the sixth Red Sox to be named American League Rookie of the year. Previous winners included position players Walt Dropo, Carlton Fisk, Fred Lynn and Nomar Garciaparra, and pitcher Don Schwall.

If you get a platinum sombrero for five strikeouts in a single game, what is it called to have six, a diamond sombrero? It has only happened eight times in MLB history, and Boston's Cecil Cooper experienced it on June 14, 1974. It took place during a 15-inning game at the California Angels.

In the Red Sox 110-year history, six father-son combinations have played for the franchise. They include Dolf and Doug Camilli, Ed Connolly Sr. and Jr., Dick and Steve Ellsworth, Walt and Allen Ripley, Haywood and Marc Sullivan, and Smokey Joe and Joe Wood.

Six hours is a long time to play ball. The longest recorded Red Sox game lasted six hours and 35 minutes. The 18-inning contest ended with the BoSox on the short end of the score – Red Sox 7, Rangers 8.

Pedro Martinez and Curt Schilling hold Boston's career postseason record for the most wins. They have six postseason wins.

By The Numbers

• • • ○ ○ ○

6

Boston Red Sox

○ ○ ○ • • •

7

BASEBALL

The Boston Red Sox have won seven World Series titles. The championship seasons took place in 1903, 1912, 1915, 1916, 1918, 2004 and 2007.

Excluding Jackie Robinson's No. 42, the BoSox have retired seven jersey numbers. They include: Bobby Doerr's No.1, Joe Cronin's No. 4, Johnny Pesky's No. 6, Carl Yastrzemski's No. 8, Ted Williams's No. 9, Jim Rice's No. 14 and Carlton Fisk's No. 27.

Boston's record for the most runs scored in an inning took place in the seventh inning of the game played against Detroit on June 18, 1953. The 17-run inning led to a 23-3 victory over the Tigers that day.

In 1997, Nomar Garciaparra hit seven leadoff home runs to set the Red Sox record for the category.

Ollie Marquardt was the first-ever Red Sox to wear jersey No. 7. Since he first donned the number in 1931, a total of 31 Red Sox have worn the number. Right fielder J.D. Drew is currently No. 7.

Jimmie Foxx, Jackie Jensen, David Ortiz, Manny Ramirez, Mo Vaughn and Carl Yastrzemski each hit seven career grand slams for the Red Sox.

The Red Sox career postseason record for the most saves is seven. Jonathan Papelbon recorded seven saves from 2005, 2007-09.

By The Numbers

• • • ○ ○ ○

Boston Red Sox

BASEBALL

The Red Sox were idle for eight days in 2001 as a result of the terrorism on 9/11. They had just been swept by the Yankees in a three-game series at New York that ended on Sept. 9. On Sept. 18, despite any bitterness about the recent sweep or the historical rivalry between the teams, the sound of "New York, New York" filled the air at Fenway Park as Boston's organist played tribute to all those who perished on 9/11.

Clyde Vollmer owns a Red Sox and MLB record (tied) for the most times facing a pitcher in a 9-inning game. It took place on June 8, 1950, versus the St. Louis Browns when he faced a pitcher eight times.

Jim Rice hit 100 or more RBIs in a season eight times in his Red Sox career. He did it in 1975, 1977-79 and 1983-86.

During his career with the Red Sox, Ted Williams hit 30 or more home runs in a single season eight times. He leads all Red Sox batters in this notable career category.

In 1999, Red Sox pitcher Pedro Martinez set a club and MLB record when he recorded 10 or more strikeouts in eight consecutive games.

From 2003-05, Johnny Damon tallied eight career postseason stolen bases. His effort earned him the Red Sox record for the category.

By The Numbers

Boston Red Sox

BASEBALL

Ted Williams was the last BoSox player to wear jersey No. 9. The number has not seen the playing field since his last game in 1960.

In 1951, the Red Sox set a club record by losing their final nine games of the regular season. This is the most consecutive losses to end a season in the team's history.

Boston has appeared in both the American League Division Series and American League Championship Series nine times. Seasons they appeared in the ALDS include 1995, 1998, 1999, 2003, 2004, 2005, 2007, 2008 and 2009. Club appearances in the ALCS took place in 1975, 1986, 1988, 1990, 1999, 2003, 2004, 2007 and 2008.

Roy Johnson, Jim Rice and Kevin Youkilis hold the Red Sox team record for the most consecutive multi-hit games in a season. Johnson's nine-game streak was in 1934, Rice's in 1978 and Youk's in 2007.

Nine players have each had 100 or more hits in the same season on five occasions in Red Sox history. It happened in 1984, 1991, 1999, 2003 and 2007.

Dom DiMaggio holds the Red Sox career record for the most opening-day starts by a center fielder. From 1941-42 and 1946-52, "The Little Professor" appeared in nine opening-day lineups for the BoSox.

By The Numbers

Boston Red Sox

BASEBALL

The Red Sox set an MLB record when on June 27, 2003, they scored 10 runs before the first out of the first inning. The game-opening rally led to a 25-8 victory at home over Florida.

Four Red Sox batters have hit 10 RBIs in a game. Rudy York was the first in 1946 at St. Louis, Norm Zauchin was the second in 1955 versus Washington, Fred Lynn was the third at Detroit in 1975 and Nomar Garciaparra was the fourth versus Seattle in 1999.

1938 was good to Jimmie Foxx. That season he had 10 multi-home run games to set the still active Red Sox record in the category.

David Ortiz jumped out to a quick start in 2006. He set the Red Sox record for the most home runs in the month of April by hitting a grand total of 10.

Cy Young and Joe Wood are the only right-handed pitchers in Red Sox history to throw 10 shutout victories.

Marco Scutaro wore jersey No. 16 in 2010. Hoping a new number would bring him good fortune, he switched to No. 10 for 2011. His favorite jersey number, No. 9, was retired by Boston in honor of Ted Williams.

Tim Wakefield owns the Red Sox career postseason pitching record for the most series played. Wakefield played in a total of 10 postseason series (1995, 1998, 1999, 2003, 2004, 2005, 2007 and 2008).

By The Numbers

Boston Red Sox

○ ○ ○ • • •

B
A
S
E
B
A
L
L

Eleven Red Sox have been named American League Most Valuable Player. This includes Tris Speaker who received the Chalmers Award in 1912.

In 1914, Red Sox pitcher Dutch Leonard took to the road with a vengeance. That season he had 11 consecutive wins on the road to set the longstanding team record for the category.

Since 1967, Red Sox batters have hit a home run from both sides of the plate in the same game 11 times. Reggie Smith did it four times, Carl Everett and Bill Mueller each did it twice and Luis Alicea, Jason Varitek and Victor Martinez have each done it once.

The most runs the BoSox have overcome to win a game are 11. Cleveland led Boston 12-1 on Aug. 28, 1950, before Boston staged an unstoppable rally, ending the game in a 15-14 victory.

Eleven managers enshrined in Cooperstown have managed the Boston Red Sox at one time in their careers.

Seven times in Red Sox history the team has gone on an 11-game winning streak. In comparison, they have experienced only three 11-game losing streaks.

On June 18, 1953, in the seventh inning of a game versus the Detroit Tigers, the Red Sox hit 11 singles to set a club record for the most singles hit in a single inning.

By The Numbers

• • • ○ ○ ○

Boston Red Sox

○○○•••

BASEBALL

The most strikeouts thrown in a no-hitter by a Red Sox pitcher are 12. Joe Wood fanned 12 St. Louis batters on July 29, 1911, in the first game of a doubleheader. Boston won the game 5-0.

Mike Higgins had 12 consecutive hits during the 1938 season. This feat not only set a Red Sox record but also ties him for the most in MLB history.

In 1909 and 1914, Tris Speaker led the league in double plays by an outfielder. Coincidentally, he had exactly 12 each season.

The Red Sox followed the 1988 All-Star break with 12 straight wins. It is the most consecutive victories following the Mid-Season Classic in team history.

Boston batters hit 12 doubles in a game at Detroit on July 29, 1990. The effort earned them both a club and an MLB record (tied).

1984 was the last season no Red Sox player or coach wore jersey No.12. The only seasons since 1931 in which No. 12 was inactive were 1978 and 1984.

David Ortiz has hit 12 home runs in postseason play for the Red Sox. He owns the club's record for the most career postseason home runs.

Hobe Ferris holds the BoSox record for the most assists by a second baseman in an extra-innings game. He had 12 in a 20-inning game on July 4, 1905 (G2) vs. the Athletics.

By The Numbers

•••○○○

12

Boston Red Sox

○ ○ ○ • • • ──────────────── 13

B
A
S
E
B
A
L
L

Ted Williams hit 13 home runs in extra innings during his 19-year career with the Red Sox.

In both 1989 and 2002, the Red Sox won 13 games by one run. This is the club's record for fewest games won by one run in a season.

Red Sox rookie George Scott was intentionally walked 13 times in 1966. No other Red Sox rookie has had more intentional walks.

Earning a Red Sox monthly home run record is no easy feat. Jim Rice set the record for the month of May with 13 in 1978. Dwight Evans and Jimmie Foxx are co-holders for the month of August with 13. Foxx hit his 13 in August 1940 and Evans hit his 13 in August 1987.

Through 2010, only 14 Red Sox players have been brave enough to wear unlucky No. 13 on their jersey. Bob Fothergill was the first in 1933. Niuman Romero is the most recent in 2010.

Tex Hughson and Dave Ferriss have both pitched 13 consecutive winning games at Fenway Park. They are co-holders of Boston's record in the category. Their individual records were set two years apart. Hughson did it in 1944, while Ferriss matched the effort in 1946.

By The Numbers

The fewest games the Red Sox have won by one run in a single season are 13 (2002 and 1989).

• • • ○ ○ ○

Boston Red Sox

○ ○ ○ • • •

B
A
Fourteen letters in Red Sox catcher Jarrod Saltalamacchia's surname makes it the longest last name in the history of MLB.

S
E
Boston's record for the most RBIs in back-to-back games was set by Rudy York in 1946. York amassed 14 RBIs in games played on July 26 and 27.

B
A
L
L
The BoSox own an American League record for the most team hits in an inning. The record was set with their 14 hits versus Detroit in the seventh inning of a game played on June 18, 1953.

Jackie Jenson and David Ortiz own the Red Sox record for the most home runs in a single month. Jenson belted 14 homers in June 1958 and Ortiz knocked 14 out of the park in July 2006.

It is challenging for a team to score 14 runs in an entire game. However, the Red Sox set a team and American League record (tied) for the most runs scored in the first inning of a ball game when on June 27, 2003 they scored 14 runs in their first at-bat versus the Florida Marlins. The prodigious start led to a 25-8 lopsided Red Sox victory.

Jim Rice wore jersey No. 14 as both a Red Sox player from 1974-89 and as a Red Sox coach from 1995-2000. The number has been retired since 2009.

Jason Varitek has played in 14 postseason series in his BoSox career. He holds the club's career record for most series played.

By The Numbers

• • • ○ ○ ○

Boston Red Sox

○○○•••

⊕15⊕

BASEBALL

The selection committee for the Boston Red Sox Hall of Fame is made up of 15 individuals. Since 1995, the committee has been responsible for selecting Hall of Fame members from the list of nominees given to them by The Sports Museum of New England and the Boston Red Sox Booster Club.

In 1946, the Red Sox won 15 consecutive games to set a team record that has stood since that season. The streak lasted from April 25 to May 10.

Roger Clemens once fanned 15 batters in a single game during his rookie season on Aug. 21, 1984. The Red Sox opponent that day was Kansas City. Clemens' effort resulted in an 11-1 victory.

Since the Red Sox were founded in 1901 the team has had 15 owners/owner groups. Charles W. Somers was the team's first, and the current group led by John Henry, Larry Lucchino and Tom Werner is the 15th.

Six times in his Red Sox career pitcher Pedro Martinez struck out 15 batters in a single game. These performances are ranked 10th overall (tied) for the most strikeouts in a single game.

Fifteen Red Sox batters have been walked in a nine-inning game on five occasions, it is a BoSox record.

The BoSox career postseason record for the most doubles hit is 15. David Ortiz hit 15 doubles in postseason appearances from 2003-05 and 2007-09.

By The Numbers

•••○○○

Boston Red Sox

○○○•••   16

B Sixteen consecutive wins by a major league
A pitcher is an extraordinary accomplishment. Red
       Sox pitcher Joe Wood did just that in 1912, and he did
       it on the road. He shares the American League record
S for the category.

E Ted Williams owns the Red Sox record for the most
B seasons with 20 or more home runs. His legendary
       visual acuity helped him accomplish this feat 16 times.
A
L On June 18, 1975, Fred Lynn amassed 16 total bases
       at Detroit to set a club record. The Red Sox enjoyed a
L 15-1 victory over the Tigers that day.

Strong relievers are critical to any team's success. In 1964, Dick Radatz earned 16 wins as a BoSox reliever. No Red Sox reliever has ever earned more.

Boston has scored 20 or more runs in a game 16 times. The team's 20-run games range (by number of Red Sox runs) from a 20-4 win versus the St. Louis Browns in 1950 to a 29-4 shellacking of those same Browns the very next day.

In the Red Sox's 161-game campaign of 1977, the team had two or more consecutive home runs in one game 16 times.

Bobby Doerr and Hobe Ferris are co-owners of the Red Sox fielding record for the most chances accepted by a second baseman in a nine-inning game. Doerr had 16 on May 30, 1946 (G2) and Ferris had 16 on May 13, 1901.

By The Numbers

•••○○○

Boston Red Sox

○ ○ ○ • • • ────────────────── 17

B
A
S
E
B
A
L
L

Ted Williams hit 17 grand slam home runs in his Red Sox career. Coincidentally, Jimmie Foxx had 17 in his major league career as well.

Russ Scarritt managed to hit 17 triples during his rookie season of 1929. His club record remains since that year.

On June 18, 1953, Boston scored 17 runs in a single inning (seventh), an American League record, versus the Detroit Tigers.

In 2006, the Red Sox set an MLB record for the most consecutive games without a team-fielding error. Through 17 games starting with their night game on June 11 to their June 30 outing, they did not commit a single fielding error.

No Red Sox pitcher hit more career home runs than Earl Wilson. Wilson hit 17 home runs from 1959-66. With six, he is also tied for the most home runs in a season by a Red Sox pitcher.

In the Red Sox record-breaking outing versus the St. Louis Browns on June 18, 1950, Boston set a club and major league high for the most extra-base hits in a game. The 17 extra-base hits remain an MLB record through 2010.

Herold "Muddy" Ruel recorded 17 double plays in 1922. This was good enough to earn him the No. 1 spot on the Red Sox single-season list for the most double plays by a catcher.

By The Numbers

• • • ○ ○ ○

Boston Red Sox

○○○••• ────────────── 18

B Ted Williams was selected to 18 All-Star Game rosters in his career.

A
S On June 17, 1920, Boston set a club record for the most walks in an extra-innings game. In 13 innings at Detroit, 18 Red Sox were walked.
E

B Eighteen combinations of relatives have played for the Red Sox since 1901. This includes brother, father-son, grandfather-son and uncle-nephew combos. The most recent pairing was brothers Pedro (1998-2004) and Ramon (1999-2000) Martinez.
A
L
L

In 1998 and 2003, the Red Sox had a record of 18-8 in the month of April. This is the best monthly record for April in club history.

The Red Sox organization notes that 18 National Baseball Hall of Famers spent significant parts of their career playing in Boston.

Eighteen hidden ball plays have been recorded by Red Sox players in the history of the franchise.

Joe Cronin had 18 pinch hits in 1943. That is the most ever in a single season by a Red Sox player.

The 1904 Red Sox set a longstanding Major League record by fielding only 18 players throughout the entire season.

The most consecutive road games lost in a single season by the BoSox are 18 (1932).

By The Numbers

•••○○○

Boston Red Sox

BASEBALL

Carl Yastrzemski holds the Red Sox record for the most All-Star Game appearances. Yaz was named to 19 All-Star teams.

The BoSox earned their best-ever winning percentage in the month of September thanks to 19 victories in September 1949. They went 19-5, for a .792 winning percentage that month.

Some team records you just want to forget. On Aug. 12, 1974, 19 Red Sox were fanned by Nolan Ryan in a 2-4 loss (nine-inning game) versus the Angels.

From July 4-25, 1996, Red Sox batters hit 30 home runs over the course of 19 consecutive games to set a club record for one or more home runs in consecutive games.

Boston's record for the most runs scored in a shutout is 19. On April 30, 1950, Boston defeated Philadelphia 19-0. Coincidentally, the largest loss in a shutout of the Red Sox was by the Cleveland Indians on May 18, 1955, by a score of 19-0.

Nineteen Red Sox batters have hit for the cycle. Of them, Leon Culberson hit for the natural cycle on July 3, 1943 and Bob Watson hit for the natural cycle on Sept. 15, 1979. Bobby Doerr is the only BoSox to ever hit for the cycle in two games.

In a nine-inning game versus Minnesota played on May 2, 1971, Boston stranded 19 runners on base to set a team record.

By The Numbers

Boston Red Sox

ooo•••

BASEBALL

Joe Cronin managed the Red Sox to 20 ties during his tenure as Boston's skipper. These are the most ties under any Red Sox manager. Bill Carrigan had the second most with 14 ties during his years at the helm.

The Red Sox have won 20 or more games 40 times in club history. The team's most recent 20-win month was in May 2007 when they went 20-8.

The number 20 also represents an inauspicious record for the BoSox: their longest losing streak. Boston lost 20 straight games from May 1-24, 2006.

In 1942, Tony Lupien set a BoSox rookie record for the fewest strikeouts in a minimum of 400 at-bats. His 20 strikeouts remain a Red Sox record through 2010.

The earliest Boston has reached 20 wins is on May 3, 1998 and 2003. The latest in a season they have reached 20 wins is July 16, 1927 and 1932.

Julio Lugo stole 20 consecutive bases in 2007, a record for consecutive stolen bases matched by no other Red Sox runner.

Dustin Pedroia stole 20 bases on 21 attempts in 2008. He led MLB with the highest stolen base percentage, .952, that season.

The most consecutive games the Red Sox have lost in a season are 20. The record was set in 1906.

By The Numbers

Boston Red Sox

BASEBALL

In June 1912 and 1961, The Red Sox won 21 games. Their overall records for the month were 21-8 and 21-13 respectively. They have never won more games than this in June.

Earl Wilson was credited with 21 wild pitches in 1963. His erratic performance also earned him first place for the most wild pitches in a season by a Red Sox pitcher.

Boston batters have had 21 team hits in a game on 12 separate occasions. The most recent occurrence was versus Tampa Bay on July 5, 2007. Boston celebrated a 15-4 victory that day.

For 21 years the Red Sox have given out the Tony Conigliaro Award. The national award honors a Major Leaguer who overcomes an obstacle and adversity. Joaquin Benoit earned this award in 2010.

The Red Sox record for the most losses by a rookie pitcher is 21. Joe Harris earned that dubious record in 1906. Coincidentally, the Red Sox record for the most wins by a rookie pitcher is also 21. Dave Ferriss earned that noteworthy record in 1945.

In 1950, Cleveland hit a record 21 home runs against Boston in 11 games played in Cleveland. In 2006, Tampa Bay equaled that total but needed 19 games in Tampa Bay to do it. These are the most home runs ever hit by a Red Sox opponent on the road.

By The Numbers

Boston Red Sox

22

On 22 occasions Boston has played in front of paid road attendance of 60,000 or more.

Carl Yastrzemski had 22 opening-day starts in his Red Sox career. This is a club record that still stands today.

Carlton Fisk and Jim Rice each hit 22 home runs during their rookie seasons as Red Sox.

In 1913, Tris Speaker hit 22 triples to set a Red Sox batting record for the category.

The club record for the most home runs by one Red Sox opponent in a season at Fenway Park is 22. In yet another coincidence, the most home runs by one opponent in a season at their home stadium is also 22. The New York Yankees own the visitor record at Fenway. They hit 22 home runs in seven games in 1977. The Kansas City A's own the road record thanks to their 22 home runs in 22 games in 1957.

On Aug. 22, 1951, the Red Sox left 22 runners on base during a 13-inning game at the St. Louis Browns. Despite abandoning a record number of base runners, Boston won the game 3-1 that day.

Stuffy McInnis set a BoSox single-game (nine innings) fielding record for the most chances accepted by a first baseman. His 22 chances accepted that game also tie him for the MLB record.

By The Numbers

Boston Red Sox

BASEBALL

In 1980, Red Sox Manager Don Zimmer wore jersey No. 23. He is the only manager to ever wear the number. Coach Herm Starrette also wore it in 1995 and 1997. Since it was first worn in 1931, a combination of 51 players, coaches and managers have worn the number. Mike Cameron is the most recent.

The winningest month of May the Red Sox have ever played was in 1978. They closed out May with a 23-7 record, for a .767 winning percentage that season.

Kevin Youkilis' longest consecutive game hitting streak in a single season is 23. He set this personal best in 2007. He is ranked 15th on the Red Sox list of 20-game consecutive hitting streaks in a single season.

A recent 20-hit game the Red Sox have had was on Aug. 23, 2009. They defeated the Baltimore Orioles 18-10 that day. Boston's 23 hits contributed to their victory versus the Orioles.

In the seventh inning of a game played on June 18, 1953, the BoSox set an MLB record with 23 plate appearances in the inning. Boston went on to win the game 23 runs to three versus the Detroit Tigers.

The record for the most home runs in a game by a Red Sox opponent is three. It has happened 23 times in club history. The most recent player to do it was Mark Teixeira on May 8, 2010, versus New York.

By The Numbers

Boston Red Sox

○○○●●●   **24**

B The largest margin of defeat Boston has ever
A experienced is 24 runs. On July 7, 1923,
       Cleveland handed the Red Sox a 3-27 loss in the first
       game of the day's doubleheader.
S
E A club record set in a game versus the Detroit Tigers
       on June 18, 1953, is for the most singles in a Red Sox
B game. Boston hit 24 singles in the 23-3 route of the
       Tigers.
A
L In 1980, Red Sox LHP Tom Burgmeier amassed 24
       saves to set the club record for the most saves by a
L left-handed pitcher.

Philadelphia took Boston deep into a 24-inning contest on Sept. 1, 1906. Remarkably, Joe Harris pitched all 24 innings for the Americans. He pitched 20 scoreless innings during the game, innings 4-23. Philadelphia rallied in the 24th to take a 4-1 victory.

In 2009, 24 Red Sox batters hit at least one home run. Their collective efforts were rewarded with a club and American League record in the category.

Red Sox legend Cy Young once pitched 24 consecutive hitless innings. His MLB and club record streak was in 1904.

The Red Sox record for the most consecutive games won at home is also an American League record. In 1988, Boston won 24 consecutive home games.

By The Numbers

●●●○○○

Boston Red Sox

25

BASEBALL

The largest margin of victory by the Red Sox in a game is 25 runs. Boston defeated St. Louis 29-4 on June 8, 1950.

The Red Sox have had 25 players who played every game of a regular season. Collectively they played 43 complete seasons between them. Right-fielder Dwight Evans was the most recent player to do it. He played every game of the 1984 season. He played every game of 1981-82 as well.

On Sept. 24, 1940, at Philadelphia, the Red Sox set a club record for the most total bases in an inning. In the sixth inning Boston had 25 total bases.

Tris Speaker had 25 career inside-the-park home runs, setting a Red Sox record. "The Grey Eagle" played for Boston from 1907-15.

The Red Sox record for the most consecutive games in a season with one or more double plays is 25. The team had 38 double plays during the 25-game streak in 1951.

In 1943, Joe Cronin had 25 RBIs as a pinch hitter. His production set not only a club record but an MLB record that still stands today.

Featured Figure

Since 1901, a total of 1,625 players have suited up for the Red Sox.

By The Numbers

Boston Red Sox

BASEBALL

On April 26, 1912, Hugh Bradley hit the first-ever home run at Fenway Park. The ball sailed over the left field wall, marking the historic moment. It would be Bradley's second and last Major League homer.

The Red Sox club record for the most shutouts won in a single season is 26. They set the mark in 1918.

In 26 games played in May of 2006 David Ortiz had 35 RBIs. In 26 games played in August of 2005 he had 30 RBIs. He is the only currently active Red Sox player on the team's list of players with 30-RBI months (since 1970).

Dave Ferriss and George Winter co-own the Red Sox Rookie record for the most complete games pitched. Ferriss had 26 complete games in 1945 and Winter had 26 in 1901.

In 1973 and 1977, Carlton Fisk had 26 home runs per season. These are the most home runs ever by a Red Sox catcher in a single season.

No Red Sox player has worn jersey No. 26 since 2004. The most recent player to don the number was Ramiro Mendoza in 2003-04.

With an errorless streak in 626 consecutive chances from June 1 through Oct. 3, 2004, Jason Varitek set the Red Sox record by a catcher for the category.

By The Numbers

Boston Red Sox

○ ○ ○ • • •   27

B On Oct. 27, 2004, the Red Sox ended their
A 86-year World Series drought. Their emphatic 4-
     0 World Series sweep of the St. Louis Cardinals
     announced their return to the top of Major League
S Baseball.

E
     The Cleveland Indians scored 27 runs on the Red Sox
B on July 7, 1923. The definitive win set a record for the
     most runs scored against the Red Sox by an opponent.
A
L The most home runs ever hit by a Red Sox second
     baseman in a season is 27. Bobby Doerr did it twice, in
L 1948 and 1950. He also owns the record for the most
     home runs in a career by a Red Sox second baseman,
     221.

On July 8, 1902, the Boston Americans had 27 hits versus Philadelphia. The Athletics had 18 hits of their own. The combined total of 45 hits set an enduring Red Sox record for the most hits by both teams in a single game.

Carlton "Pudge" Fisk's jersey No. 27 was retired on Sept. 4, 2000. Highlights of his 24-year career include 351 career home runs as a catcher, 2,226 games behind the plate, 1,330 RBIs and 5,111 putouts, just to name a few.

The 1906 Boston Americans allowed 27 inside-the-park home runs.

By The Numbers

• • • ○ ○ ○

Boston Red Sox

○○○●●●

BASEBALL

On two occasions Red Sox batters have totaled 28 hits in a single game. The first was on June 8, 1950, in a 29-4 victory over the St. Louis Browns. The second was a 25-8 victory on June 27, 2003, over the Florida Marlins at Fenway Park.

Boston used 28 pitchers throughout their 2006 campaign. This is the most pitchers ever used by the team in a single season.

Twenty-eight times in 1906 the Boston Americans were shut out by an opponent. This contrasts markedly to the fewest times the team has been shut out in a season, one in 1995.

In May 2009, Jason Bay led the Red Sox with 30 RBIs for the month. They were hit in 28 games played.

The Boston Americans were 14-14 in one-run games in 1901. The 28 one-run games are the fewest for the team in a season.

In 2003, opposing pitchers intentionally walked Manny Ramirez 28 times. He also had 97 bases on balls in his 679 plate appearances. The 28 IBBs are the second most in Red Sox history.

Fred Lynn owns the Red Sox record for the most home runs in a season at Fenway Park by a left-handed batter. He hit a record of 28 homers there in 1979. Red Sox fielders have turned a total of 29 triple plays since 1901.

By The Numbers

●●●○○○

28

Boston Red Sox

○ ○ ○ • • •

BASEBALL

On April 29, 1986, Roger Clemens made MLB history when he struck out 20 Seattle Mariners in a nine-inning game. Not one to rest on his laurels, Clemens fanned 20 Detroit Tigers in a game held a decade later. He's the only pitcher in MLB history to have two 20-strikeout nine-inning games to his credit.

Johnny Damon suited up for Boston from 2002-05. In his final season as a Red Sox he strung together a hitting streak of 29 consecutive games. No Red Sox batter has a longer streak in a season since the turn of this century (2000s).

The Red Sox record for the most extra-base hits in the postseason is held by David Ortiz. Since his first postseason appearance with the BoSox in 2003 he has tallied 29 extra-base hits.

The most runs ever scored by Boston in a game are 29. On June 8, 1950, Boston defeated St. Louis 29-4 to set the lasting mark. Chronic overachievers, the Red Sox also set their club record for RBIs in a game that day. In yet another coincidence, the record is 29 RBIs.

Featured Figure

Kevin Youkilis has recorded 429 career double plays. Youk has played for Boston since 2004. He is ranked 7th of all time on the Red Sox career list for the most double plays by a first baseman.

By The Numbers

Boston Red Sox

BASEBALL

Nomar Garciaparra had a 30-game hitting streak during his rookie season of 1997 to set the Red Sox rookie record for the category.

In 1977, Butch Hobson set the Red Sox record of 30 for the most home runs by a third baseman in a single season.

Since 1970, 22 Red Sox batters have hit 30 or more RBIs in a single month.

The earliest Boston ever reached 30 wins in a season was May 20 in 2002. The latest the team ever reached 30 wins was Aug. 18 in 1932.

Mike Timlin is credited with 30 career relief wins. Timlin played for six seasons in Boston from 2003-08. His 30 relief wins are good enough to earn him the No. 7 position on the Red Sox career leaders' list for the category.

Featured Figure

Red Sox players have hit .300 or higher in a season 187 times. The highest-ever batting average was .406 by none other than Ted Williams in 1941. Williams is second on the list as well with a .388 batting average in 1957. The most recent Red Sox players to eclipse .300 for a season are Adrian Beltre, Victor Martinez and Kevin Youkilis in 2010. They had a .312, .307 and .302 batting average respectively.

By The Numbers

Boston Red Sox

○ ○ ○ • • • �31

B
A
S
E
B
A
L
L

The Red Sox hold MLB's modern-day record for the most times scoring 10 or more runs in a single inning. The team has accomplished this feat 31 times in the modern era.

In 1914, Duffy Lewis was caught stealing 31 times. He set a Red Sox record for the most times caught stealing in a single season. His record stands today.

Six times in club history a Red Sox hitter has amassed 31 RBIs in a single month. This includes Jim Rice (Sept. 1980), Dwight Evans (Aug. 1987), Mike Greenwell (June 1988), John Valentin (Aug. 1995), Manny Ramirez (April 2001) and David Ortiz (June 2004).

Left-handed pitcher Jon Lester currently wears jersey No. 31. He is the 42 Red Sox to wear the number. He's worn it since the 2007 season. It is, however, not the only jersey number he's worn while playing for the Red Sox. He wore No. 62 during his rookie season, 2006, when Coach Brad Mills wore the No. 31.

Bob Unglaub owns a Red Sox fielding record for the most putouts in an extra-innings game. On July 4, 1905, Unglaub had 31 putouts in a 20-inning contest (game two) versus the Philadelphia Athletics (Boston 2, Philadelphia 4).

The 1943 Red Sox set an MLB record for the most extra-innings games in a season thanks to their 31 extra-innings outings that season.

By The Numbers

• • • ○ ○ ○

Boston Red Sox

David Ortiz led all Red Sox hitters with 32 home runs in 2010. Coincidentally, Ortiz owns an American League single-season record for the most home runs on the road – 32 in 2006.

Dennis Boyd (1986), John Tudor (1983), Luis Tiant (1973) and Bill Monbouquette (1965) have each led a Red Sox pitching staff with 32 home runs allowed in a season.

In baseball, the term "chances accepted" refers to the total number of putouts and assists by a fielder. Bob Unglaub set a Red Sox record for the most chances accepted in an extra-innings game. His record was set on July 4, 1905, in game two of a doubleheader versus the Philadelphia Athletics, a 2-4 Boston loss. His 32 total chances accepted are derived from his 31 putouts and single assist earned during that game.

Featured Figure

1932 was not a banner year for the Boston Red Sox. They ended the season with a disappointing 43-111 overall record. The resulting .279 winning percentage is the lowest in team history of all time. The team's winningest month was July. Their 32 games played that month resulted in a 14-18 record, for a .438 winning percentage. The 1932 team could only manage a winning record against one opponent that season. Their season split with the Chicago White Sox was 12-10, for a .545 winning percentage.

Boston Red Sox

○○○•••

(33)

B
A
S
Red Sox batters have earned the American League Silver Slugger Award 33 times. The first Red Sox to receive the award were Carney Lansford and Dwight Evans in 1981. The most recent recipient was Adrian Beltre in 2010.

E
B
A
In additional to his many Red Sox batting records, Ted Williams also had 33 career pinch hits. He is ranked 4th of all time on the Red Sox career list for the category.

L
L
Tim Wakefield allowed 33 bases on balls during his postseason play for the Red Sox. He owns the team's record for the category.

In 1902, Cy Young led the league with a 33-10 record. He set a club record that stood for 11 seasons until Joe Wood's 34-5 season in 1912. Wood's record remains the Red Sox record to this day.

John Lackey led all Red Sox pitchers with 33 games started in 2010. It was the fifth time in his professional career that he had 33 starts in a season.

In 1957, Ted Williams was walked intentionally 33 times. No other Red Sox hitter has ever been intentionally walked more in a single season.

Since 1901, Boston has hit into 33 triple plays. The most recent occurrence was on Aug. 6, 2001, versus Texas when Scott Hatteberg hit into the triple play in the fourth inning.

By The Numbers

•••○○○

Boston Red Sox

B A S E B A L L

Carl Everett set the Red Sox single-season record for the most home runs as a switch hitter in 2000. He had 34 homers that year.

In 1950, Walt Dropo hit 34 home runs to set the club record for the most home runs by a Red Sox rookie.

The Red Sox record for the most consecutive games with a hit in a season is held by Dom DiMaggio. In 1949, he had at least one hit in 34 consecutive games. The streak ended on Aug. 9 at Fenway when he hit a line drive to center field to his older brother, Joe DiMaggio.

Carl Yastrzemski had 34 game-tying and go-ahead RBIs in 1972. It was the first of three non-consecutive seasons that he would lead the team in the category. In a coincidence, David Ortiz's first season leading the team in the category was with 34 in 2003. Seven times he has led the team in the category, 2003-08 and 2010.

The most wins in a season by a right-handed pitcher in Red Sox history is Joe Wood. His 34 wins in 1912 remain a club record through the 2010 season.

Featured Figure

Twenty-two position players have pitched 32 times in Red Sox history. Bill Hall was the most recent. Hall pitched one inning on May 28, 2010, versus Kansas City. The game ended with Boston on the short end of a 5-12 score.

By The Numbers

Boston Red Sox

BASEBALL

Tris speaker set a Red Sox single-season fielding record for outfielders in 1909 with 35 assists. Three years later, in 1912, he repeated his performance of 35. He led the league in assists by an outfielder both seasons.

In 1987, Red Sox pitcher Bruce Hurst set a team record for the most home runs allowed in a season by a left-handed pitcher. Thirty-five home runs were hit off Hurst that season.

Three Red Sox runners have recorded 35 stolen bases in a single season. Patsy Dougherty was the first in 1903. Tris Speaker had 35 in 1909 and 1910.

Jimmie Foxx hit 35 home runs at Fenway in 1938. His mark still stands as a Red Sox record for the most home runs at home in a season.

The most saves in a single season by a Red Sox pitcher are 35. The record was set in 2006 by Jonathan Papelbon.

In the 1953 season Boston won 35 games by one run. This remains the team's record for the most games won by one run in a single season. That same season the team lost 16 games by one run.

Kevin Youkilis set the club record for the most consecutive games in a season without an error by a BoSox first baseman from April 2 through Sept. 30, 2007. Youkilis had 135 errorless games during the streak.

By The Numbers

35

Boston Red Sox

○○○•••

36

B
A
S
E
B
A
L
L

The Red Sox record for the most home runs hit by an opponent in a season is 36. In 1954, the Cleveland Indians hit 36 home runs versus the Red Sox in 20 games played.

In 1997, the Red Sox set a team record for the most passed balls recorded in a single season. Their 36 passed balls in 162 games played remains a team record to this day.

The 1930 Red Sox lost 36 games by one run, to set an enduring team record for the category. By contrast, they only won 17 games by one run that same season.

The most combined runs scored by both teams in a Red Sox game are 36. This is an American League record and has happened twice in club history. The first time was on June 29, 1950, at Philadelphia (Boston 22, Philadelphia 14). The second time was on Aug. 12, 2008, versus Texas (Boston 19, Texas 17).

The most home runs hit in a single season by a Red Sox right fielder are 36. Tony Conigliaro hit the 36 homers in the 1970 season.

On Aug. 15, 1922, the Red Sox and Chicago White Sox hit a combined total 36 singles to set a Major League record. The White Sox hit 21 and the Red Sox hit 15.

Roxy Walters collected 36 career double plays from 1919-23. He ranks 8th of all time for Red Sox catchers in the category.

By The Numbers

•••○○○

36

Boston Red Sox

○○○•••

B
A
S
E
B
A
L
L

37

Since 1957, 37 Gold Glove awards have been awarded to Red Sox players. The most recent player to receive the honor was second baseman Dustin Pedroia for his play in 2008. That season Pedroia had 733 defensive chances, 279 putouts, 448 assists, 101 double plays and only six errors, for a .992 fielding percentage en route to earning his Gold Glove Award.

Ted Williams holds the Red Sox record for the most multi-home run games in a career. Williams had 37 multi-home runs games from 1939-42 and 1946-60.

Ted Williams' famous 502-foot home run traveled all the way to Row 37 of Section 42 at Fenway Park on June 9, 1946. The ball hit Joseph Boucher, seated in Seat 21, directly on top of the head. It reportedly bounced 12 rows higher after its initial impact.

Jason Bay hit 37 game-tying and go-ahead RBIs in 2009. Who knows how many times he might have led the team in the category had he not been traded to the Mets following the 2009 season?

Featured Figure

On Opening Day 2010 more than 37,000 fans packed New Yankee Stadium to watch the Red Sox-Yankees rivalry game. More precisely, 37,440 fans were in attendance that night. It set a new record for opening-day attendance for the Red Sox franchise. The Red Sox spoiled the Yankees' inaugural opening-day party at New Yankee Stadium by taking a 9-7 victory from the Yankees.

By The Numbers

•••○○○

Boston Red Sox

B
A
S
Bobby Doerr and Ted Williams homered 38 times in the same game during their careers with the Red Sox. This places them in 3rd place on the list of top pairs of Red Sox teammates homering in the same game.

E
B
A
In 2003, Red Sox batters hit 38 home runs in 19 games versus the Baltimore Orioles to set a team record for the most home runs hit in a season versus one opponent.

L
L
Right-handed pitcher Bob Stanley was credited with 38 double plays in his Red Sox career (1977-89). This is the most by any Red Sox pitcher.

In 1996 Tim Wakefield pitched 38 home runs. He set a Red Sox record that season for the most home runs by a right-handed pitcher in a single season.

Cy Young and Roger Clemens co-hold the Red Sox record for the most shutouts in a career, pitching 38 shutouts from 1901-08 and 1984-96 respectively.

The most home runs hit by a Red Sox center fielder in a single season are 38. Fred Lynn hit 38 in 1979 and Tony Armas hit 38 in 1984.

The Red Sox career record for the most consecutive games in an errorless streak by a first baseman is 238. Kevin Youkilis set the record from July 5, 2006 through June 6, 2008.

By The Numbers

Boston Red Sox

○○○••• ⊕ 39

BASEBALL

Although jersey numbers were first worn by Red Sox players in 1931, the No. 39 was not used until 1946. The first-ever player to don the number was Eddie Pellagrini, who claimed No. 39 for two seasons, 1946-47.

In part, thanks to his 39 home runs, Mo Vaughn earned the American League Most Valuable Player award in 1995. He also had 126 RBIs and a .300 batting average that season en route to winning the award.

The Red Sox career postseason record for the most runs scored is 39. David Ortiz scored a combined total 39 runs from 2003-05 and 2007-09.

For Game 3 of the 2008 American League Division Series, just over 39,000 spectators filled Fenway Park to see the Red Sox take on Los Angeles. The Angels stole a 5-4 victory from Boston in front of the postseason single-game record-setting crowd. Attendance was officially recorded at 39,067.

Through the 2010 season, Dustin Pedroia has been credited with 339 double plays. This ranks him 9th on the Red Sox career list for second basemen.

Featured Figure

April 20, 1939, marked the Major League debut of Red Sox legend Ted Williams. In what can be considered an inauspicious start to his hall-of-fame career, Williams had just one hit, zero RBIs and scored no runs in his four at-bats that day.

By The Numbers

•••○○○

Boston Red Sox

○○○ ••• 　　　　　　　　　　　　　　　　40

BASEBALL

Boston has celebrated forty 20-win months in team history. The first 20-win month was in June 1901, when the team went 20-5. The most recent was May 2007, when they earned a 20-8 month-long record.

Carl Yastrzemski is the only member of the Red Sox 20-Homers / 20-Steals club who hit 40 or more home runs while qualifying for the club. Yaz had 23 stolen bases along with 40 home runs in 1970 to qualify for the exclusive club. There are only five Red Sox players who have hit 20 or more homers and had 20 or more steals in a season.

The earliest date the Red Sox have won their 40th game of the season was on June 6, 2002. The latest they have ever won their 40th game was on Sept. 13, 1925.

Rico Petrocelli holds the Red Sox record for the most home runs hit by a shortstop in a single season. In 1969 Petrocelli hit 40 home runs to set the club record.

The only two Red Sox players to ever hit exactly 40 RBIs in a single month are Ted Williams and Clyde Vollmer. Williams hit 40 in June 1950 (29 games) and Vollmer hit 40 in July 1951 (29 games).

Rick Burleson holds down the No. 2 spot on the Red Sox career list for the most assists by a shortstop. "Rooster" amassed 3,240 assists from 1974-80.

By The Numbers

••• ○○○

Boston Red Sox

○○○•••

41

BASEBALL

Jim Rice had 41 combined game-tying and go-ahead RBIs in 1979. Manny Ramirez had 41 in 2004. They are the only two Red Sox to ever hit 40 or more in a season without leading the team for that year.

Ted Williams' 41 RBIs in May 1942 are the most RBIs in a single month by any Red Sox hitter. The RBIs were hit in 28 games played that month.

Perhaps more known for his hitting than pitching, it may surprise you that Babe Ruth still holds the Red Sox record for the most starts by a left-handed pitcher in a season. He had 41 starts in 1916.

The 1995 Boston Red Sox set a club record for the most players making their first appearance for the team in a single season. Forty-one Red Sox players made their Red Sox debut that season.

In 1902, Cy Young set Boston's record for the most complete games pitched with 41. He also owns the 2nd and 4th spots in the category as well with 40 in 1904 and 38 in 1901 respectively.

1941 was a great year for Ted Williams. Amongst his accomplishments that season are his .428 club record single-season home batting average and .380 club record single-season road batting average.

The Red Sox career postseason record for the most bases on balls is 41. David Ortiz set the record from 2003-05 and 2007-09.

By The Numbers

•••○○○

Boston Red Sox

○ ○ ○ • • •

B
A
S
E
B
A
L
L

On April 15, 1947, Jackie Robinson made his debut with the Brooklyn Dodgers. His courage in breaking baseball's color barrier was honored by all 30 MLB teams in 1997. The No. 42 was retired simultaneously by all big league franchises, including the Boston Red Sox. Coach DeMarlo Hale, Coco Crisp and David Ortiz all wore No. 42 to honor Robinson on April 22, 2007. The entire Red Sox roster wore No. 42 on April 15, 2009 and on the same date once again in 2010 to honor the legend on the league's now annual "Jackie Robinson Day."

In 2000, Derek Lowe had 42 saves. His performance tied him for the league lead. It also ranks him 2nd on the Red Sox list of single-season saves leaders of all time.

"Oil Can" Boyd sits atop Boston's single-season list for the most putouts by a pitcher. In 1985, he led the team and the league with 42 putouts.

The namesake of "Pesky's Pole," Johnny Pesky, began his career with the Red Sox in 1942. He played for Boston in 1942, and again from 1946-52. Pesky's jersey No. 6 was retired by Boston in 2008.

Butch Hobson had 1,042 assists from 1975-80. The most assists he ever had in a single season were 272 in 1977. He is ranked 7th of all time on the Red Sox career list for the most career assists by a third baseman.

By The Numbers

Boston Red Sox

43

B
A
S
E
B
A
L
L

The most home runs Ted Williams ever hit in a single season as a Red Sox is 43. He had 43 home runs to lead the team and league in 1949.

Tom Gordon owns the franchise record for the most consecutive saves in a single season. Gordon collected 43 consecutive saves in 1998 to set the mark.

The Red Sox career postseason record for the most runs batted in is 43. This is one of many career postseason records owned by Big Papi.

Cy Young's single-season pitching record for the most starts by a right-hander has stood since 1902. That season he amassed 43 starts to set the Red Sox record.

Russ Nixon rounds out the top three Red Sox with the most career pinch hits. In a single season with Boston, 1968, Nixon had 43 pinch hits.

Jersey No. 43 has been worn by 21 Red Sox players and coaches since its first use in 1952. Coach George Susce was the first to don the number from 1952-54. Matt Fox was the most recent player to wear it in 2010.

Jim Rice played 1,543 career games for Boston. This is the 5th highest total of all time by any Red Sox outfielder.

By The Numbers

Boston Red Sox

○ ○ ○ • • •

BASEBALL

On the strength of his 44 home runs, 121 RBIs and .326 batting average in 1967, Cark Yastrzemski was named the American League Most Valuable Player.

Through the 2010 season, the Red Sox have a 3,626-3,044 all-time record. This gives them MLB's second best all-time winning percentage of .544.

Red Sox great Joe Cronin hit 44 triples in his career at Boston. His major league total was 118.

Since its inception in 1967, 44 Red Sox players have earned the BoSox Club Man of the Year Award. The first honoree was shortstop Rico Petrocelli in 1967. Right-handed pitcher Clay Buchholz was the 2010 recipient.

The Red Sox total road game attendance has topped 1 million for 44 consecutive seasons. Twenty-four of those years it exceeded 2 million. Overall road attendance in 2010 was 2,615,214.

The Red Sox have had 44 all-time managers. Jimmy Collins was their first in 1901-06. The 44th is Terry Francona, who made his managerial debut with the Red Sox in 2004.

Pete Daley had an errorless streak in 144 consecutive games played from June 13, 1956 through Sept. 10, 1958. This is the career record by a Red Sox catcher.

By The Numbers

• • • ○ ○ ○

Boston Red Sox

○ ○ ○ • • •

BASEBALL

Boston and Philadelphia set an American League record on July 8, 1902, when they combined for 45 hits in a 27-18 Philadelphia victory. The 45 combined hits remains a Red Sox record for the most hits by both clubs in a game.

David Ortiz led the Red Sox in 2010 with 45 game-tying and go-ahead RBIs. It was the seventh time he led the team in the category.

Manny Ramirez hit 45 home runs in 2005. It was the most home runs he had ever hit in a single season as a Red Sox. It also earned him the record for the most home runs hit by a Red Sox left fielder.

Second on the list for the most double plays by a Red Sox third baseman is Frank Malzone. In 1961, Malzone had 45 double plays to earn his place on that list.

In 1945, Dave Ferriss had an 11-6 record at home and a 10-4 record on the road. His is one of only five Red Sox pitchers since 1945 to win 10 or more games in a season both at home and on the road.

Featured Figure

Since its inception in 1933, the only season an MLB All-Star Game was not held was in 1945. Due to World War II the game was cancelled, but MLB held a series of replacement games, including one at Fenway Park. The game between the Braves and the Red Sox raised $70,000 for the United War Fund. The Red Sox defeated the Braves 8-1 that day.

By The Numbers

Boston Red Sox

○ ○ ○ ● ● ●

46

B
A
S
E
B
A
L
L

Tris Speaker once stole 46 bases in a season. The year was 1913. It was the second most steals he ever had in a season, behind his 52 the preceding season. He is ranked 3rd and 5th of all time on the Red Sox single season list.

In 1998, Tom "Flash" Gordon had 46 saves. The saves helped him secure the Red Sox single-season record for the most saves by a right-handed pitcher and his first All-Star selection.

Jim Rice led the Red Sox and MLB with 46 home runs in 1978. The performance ranks him 4th of all time on Boston's single-season home runs list.

The MLB record for the most players used by both clubs in a single nine-inning game is 46. It was none other than the Red Sox and Yankees who set the record in a game held on Oct. 2, 2005. New York won that game 24-22.

The 2nd most at-bats in a season without a home run in Red Sox history are 646. Tom Oliver did, however, hit 46 RBIs during those at-bats in 1930.

Featured Figure

The all-time record for the most hits in an All-Star Game is 4. Two Red Sox players co-hold the record with Joe Medwick. Ted Williams hit two singles and two home runs on July 9, 1946, at Fenway Park. Carl Yastrzemski hit a double and three singles on July 14, 1970. Yaz earned the Outstanding Player of the Game for his performance.

By The Numbers

● ● ● ○ ○ ○

Boston Red Sox

○○○••• ───────────── 47

B
A
S
E
B
A
L
L

The Red Sox skipper himself, Terry Francona, currently wears jersey No. 47. He never wore the number during his playing days, opting for No. 16 (Expos and Cubs), No. 10 (Reds), No. 24 (Indians) and No. 30 (Brewers).

The Red Sox Rookie record for the most doubles hit in a single season is 47. The record is held by Fred Lynn. He hit 47 doubles in 1975.

The most home runs ever hit in a season by a Red Sox designated hitter is 47. Designated hitter David Ortiz set the mark in 2006.

From April 11-Sept. 27, 1928, Ed Morris set the Red Sox record for the longest errorless streak by a starting pitcher in a single season. Morris had 47 errorless games during that stretch.

The 1912 Boston Red Sox finished the season with a 105-47 regular-season record. The resulting .691 winning percentage is the highest ever recorded by a Red Sox team.

Featured Figure

The largest crowd on record to ever see a Red Sox game in Boston is 47,627. On Sept. 22, 1935, the 47 thousand-plus fans watched the Red Sox play the Yankees in a doubleheader at Fenway Park. As fortune would have it for those Red Sox fans in attendance that record-setting day, the Red Sox dropped both games to the Yankees, 2-5 (Game 1) and 4-6 (Game 2).

By The Numbers

•••○○○

Boston Red Sox

○ ○ ○ ● ● ●

48

B
A
S
E
B
A
L
L

Boston's record for the highest winning percentage on the road was set in 1912. That season, the team had a 48-27 road record, for a .640 winning percentage.

During their playing years together, the Red Sox duo of David Ortiz and Manny Ramirez hit 48 home runs in the same game. They are ranked 2nd of all time on the list of top pairs of Red Sox teammates homering in the same game.

Tim Wakefield owns the Red Sox career record for the most earned runs allowed in the postseason. He allowed 48 earned runs in postseason play (1995, 1998-99, 2003-05 and 2007-09).

Johnny Pesky had 48 double plays in 1949. The effort helped him secure the Red Sox single-season record for the most double plays by a third baseman.

No one in the Red Sox organization used jersey No. 48 until 1972. Since jersey numbers were first worn by the team in 1931, that is 41 years of inactivity for the number.

Featured Figure

Ted Williams loved Fenway, and the park loved him back. Over the course of his career Williams hit 248 home runs at Fenway Park. No other Red Sox hitter has ejected more balls from MLB's oldest ball park.

By The Numbers

● ● ● ○ ○ ○

Boston Red Sox

○ ○ ○ • • • ————————————— 49

B
A
S
E
B
A
L
L

In 2010, Adrian Beltre hit 49 doubles. He led the league and earned himself a top-10 spot on the Red Sox list for the most doubles hit in a single season.

Jim Rice hit 49 game-tying and go-ahead RBIs in 1983. He led Boston in the category six times in his career.

Second baseman Bill Wambsganss ranks 6th on the Red Sox list of all time for the most at-bats in a season without a home run. His 632 at-bats led to zero home runs in 1924. Along the way, he did manage to hit 49 RBIs, however.

The 1966 Red Sox allowed opponents to hit 49 home runs in the month of June. This still stands as the most home runs allowed in one month in club history.

The most runs Boston has scored in two consecutive games are 49. The team accomplished this feat in games versus the St. Louis Browns on June 7-8, 1950. It is an MLB record. Boston won those games 20-4 and 29-4 respectively.

Rick Miller is 2nd on the Red Sox career pinch-hit leaders list. He had 49 pinch-hits from 1971-77 and 1981-85.

The 5th highest number of games played by a Red Sox catcher is 649. Bill Carrigan played those games in 1906 and 1908-16.

By The Numbers

• • • ○ ○ ○

Boston Red Sox

○ ○ ○ • • •   ──────────────── 50

B
A
S
David Ortiz and Jimmie Foxx are the only two Red Sox to ever hit 50 or more home runs in a single season. Ortiz had 54 in 2006 and Foxx hit 50 in 1938. Foxx's 50 home runs set a record for the most home runs hit by a right-hander in Boston's history.

E
B
A
L
The Red Sox rookie record for the most stolen bases in a single season was set in 2008. Jacoby Ellsbury set that record with 50 stolen bases. This same effort also earns him the 4th spot on the club's list of players with 25 or more steals in a season.

L
Boston has never achieved 50 wins in a season prior to June 25 (1978). Conversely, the team has never achieved 50 wins later than Sept. 24 (1927).

Tim Wakefield holds the Red Sox record for the most runs allowed in the postseason. He allowed 50 runs in games played from 1995 to 2009.

Rico Petrocelli had 150 double plays during his career. He ranks 4th of all time on Boston's career leaders list for the most double plays by a third baseman.

Featured Figure

The incomparable Ted Williams ended his career his way. On Sept. 28, 1960, in the bottom of the eighth he sent a 1-1 pitch out of the park for the last at-bat of his illustrious career. Although the BoSox were heading to the Bronx for their final series of the season, Williams did not make the trip, electing to end his season and career at Fenway, with that legendary 450-foot home run.

By The Numbers

• • • ○ ○ ○

Boston Red Sox

○ ○ ○ • • •

B
A
S
E
B
A
L
L

⊕ 51

In 2007, the Red Sox bid just over $51 million to acquire Daisuke Matsuzaka. Eventually Matsuzaka signed a six-year contract worth $52 million.

The 1927 Boston Red Sox could only manage 51 wins. They finished the season with a 51-103 overall record, for a .331 winning percentage. They were 59 games back from the American League-leading Yankees.

Nomar Garciaparra, Wade Boggs and Joe Cronin each hit 51 doubles in a single season. Garciaparra hit 51 in 2000, Boggs in 1989 and Cronin in 1938. They rank 6th on the Red Sox all-time list.

Boston's second highest all-time winning percentage on the road is .630, and was earned with their 51 wins and 30 losses in 2002.

Rich Gedman is credited with 51 double plays. This ranks him 6th on the Red Sox career list for the most double plays by a catcher.

Bill Campbell rounds out the top-10 list for the most career saves for the Red Sox organization. He had 51 saves in his years with the club from 1977-81.

Featured Figure

The highest-ever average home attendance for Red Sox spring training is 7,751. The record average attendance was set through 16 home games played in 2005's spring training.

By The Numbers

• • • ○ ○ ○

Boston Red Sox

○ ○ ○ • • •

B
A
S
E

Tris Speaker had 52 stolen bases in 1912. His quick feet and superior timing place him 3rd on Boston's list of players with 25 or more steals in a season. Further, in his nine seasons in Boston, Speaker accumulated 267 total stolen bases. In his entire 22-year major league career, he recorded 436, for a 162-game average of 25.

B
A
L
L

The Red Sox list of most at-bats without a home run in a season includes Billy Goodman. Second baseman Goodman had 599 at-bats in 1955 with no home runs. He did, however, manage to contribute by hitting 52 RBIs in those at-bats.

In 2007, David Ortiz hit 52 doubles. He is ranked 5th on the Red Sox list of single-season batting leaders in the category of most doubles.

Since 1975, Red Sox players have won 52 American League Player or Pitcher of the Month honors. DH David Ortiz (May 2010), LHP Jon Lester (May 2010) and RHP Clay Buchholz (August 2010) are the most recent recipients.

Featured Figure

George Scott set an undesirable mark in 1966 when he struck out 152 times as a rookie. He leads all Red Sox rookies with that performance. During his 9-year career with the BoSox Scott accumulated 850 total strikeouts. His 162-game MLB career average was 113 strikeouts.

By The Numbers

• • • ○ ○ ○

Boston Red Sox

BASEBALL

In 2010, the Red Sox used 53 players in the regular season. The same number of players was used in 2006 and 1995.

The Red Sox team pitching record for most saves in a single season is 53. The record was set in 1998.

Johnny Pesky and Dom DiMaggio are co-holders of Boston's single-season record for the most hits in a month. Pesky had 53 hits in August 1946 and DiMaggio had 53 in August 1950.

The third largest-ever winning margin for the Red Sox was achieved in a 1953 game versus Detroit. The Red Sox defeated the Tigers 23-3 on June 18, 1953. Five single-inning club records were set in this game. They include: most batters facing a pitcher in one inning (23), most runs scored by a team in one inning (17), most hits by a team in one inning (14), most singles by a team in one inning (11) and most batters on a team reaching first base in one inning (20). Additionally, Sammy White set a record for the most runs scored in one inning (3) and Gene Stephens set one for the most hits in one inning (3).

Ted Williams had an on-base percentage of .553 in 1941. His record-setting performance remains unequalled by any other Red Sox to this day.

Jim Tabor is ranked 3rd of all time on the Red Sox career fielding leaders list for the most double plays by a third baseman. Tabor racked up 153 double plays from 1938-44.

By The Numbers

Boston Red Sox

○○○ • • • —————————————— 54

B
A
S
E
B
A
L
L

Fifty-four home runs in a season is no small feat. David Ortiz's 2006 record-setting performance remains the standard by which all Red Sox sluggers will be measured.

Jack Barry had 54 sacrifice hits in 1917. He set a Red Sox record that has stood since that season.

Red Sox legend Bobby Doerr had 54 stolen bases in his career. Although not a team record, his performance is impressive when considered with his total body of work, which also includes: 223 home runs, 1,247 RBIs, 223 hits, and 1,094 runs from 7,093 at-bats.

Tommy Harper was a prolific base-stealer. In 1973, he stole 54 total bases to earn himself the No. 2 spot on the Red Sox all-time list for the most stolen bases in a single season.

In 2008, Justin Pedroia hit 54 doubles. His success at hitting doubles that season led to his No. 3 ranking on Boston's single-season leaders list for the category.

The Red Sox and American League single-season pitching record for the most consecutive saves for any season is held by Tom Gordon, who from April 19, 1998, to May 31, 1999, accumulated 54 saves.

Bill Carrigan is ranked 2nd of all time for the most assists by a Red Sox catcher. Carrigan accumulated 854 assists in 1906 and from 1908-16.

By The Numbers

• • • ○○○

Boston Red Sox

○ ○ ○ • • • ⊕ 55

B
A
Red Sox batters once hit 55 home runs in one month. The year was 2003 in the month of July. They set a team record unequalled to this day.

S
E
Fifty-five players used in a season is the club's record. In 1996, Boston played 55 players throughout the regular season.

B
A
L
L
Dalton Jones currently holds the Red Sox record for the most career pinch hits. He set the club record with 55 pinch hits from 1964-69.

If you include the strike-interrupted season of 1981, the latest date the Red Sox have earned their 55th victory is Sept. 23. Not including that season, it is the Sept. 21 (1929).

Jackie Jensen won a share of the American League RBI title in 1955. He and Detroit's Ray Boon each had 116 RBIs that season. Jenson won the title again in 1958 and 1959.

The Thomas A. Yawkey Red Sox Most Valuable Player Award was given to Ted Williams in 1955. It was the 4th and final time he was given the award at the annual dinner.

The Red Sox record for the most career putouts by an outfielder is 4,255. The record was set by Dwight Evans from 1972-90.

By The Numbers

• • • ○ ○ ○

Boston Red Sox

BASEBALL

The most runs the Red Sox have ever scored in three consecutive games are 56. From June 7-9, 1950, the Red Sox outscored the St. Louis Browns 56-20 in the three-game series at Fenway. Boston won the series 2-1.

From 1924-30 Phil Todt hit 56 triples for the Red Sox. Todt, more known for his defensive specialty, is still ranked 3rd of all time on MLB's single-season list for range factor by a first baseman. Todt's highest range factor of 12.210 was achieved in 1926.

Nomar Garciaparra hit 56 doubles in 2002. He led the league along with Garret Anderson of the Anaheim Angels. His 56 doubles were also good enough to place him 2nd on Boston's all-time list for the most doubles hit in a season.

Dwight Evans and Jim Rice sit atop Boston's list of top pairs of Red Sox teammates homering in the same game. Fifty-six times the duo homered in the same game.

Fifty-six career postseason strikeouts put Jason Varitek in the undesirable lead in the category.

Harry Hooper ranks 2nd on the BoSox all-time list for the most double plays by an outfielder. Hooper recorded a total of 56 double plays in his Red Sox career from 1909-20.

By The Numbers

Boston Red Sox

○ ○ ○ • • •

BASEBALL

Ted Williams owns the Red Sox record for the most 3+ home runs in one season. He accomplished this rare feat in 1957. The record-setting homers came in games played on May 8, 1957, a 4-1 win at the Chicago White Sox and on June 13, 1957, a 9-3 win at the Cleveland Indians.

The Red Sox single-season and career records for the longest errorless streak by a shortstop are held by Alex Gonzalez. In 2006, Gonzalez had 57 consecutive games from April 11 to June 30 without an error.

David Ortiz owns the Red Sox record for the most career hits in the postseason. In postseason play from 2003 to 2009 Ortiz has managed 57 total hits to set the club record.

Dom DiMaggio hit 57 triples in his Red Sox career. DiMaggio, "The Little Professor," played for Boston from 1940-42 and 1946-53. DiMaggio, Bobby Doerr and Detroit's Hoot Evers led the AL with 11 triples in 1950.

The second most assists by a Red Sox first baseman in a single season is 157. Bill Buckner set that mark in the 1986 season.

Harry Hooper sits in the No. 6 spot for the most career putouts by a Red Sox outfielder. Hooper recorded 2,757 putouts from 1909-20.

By The Numbers

Boston Red Sox

○○○•••

58

B
A
S
E
B
A
L
L

Boston endured the curse of the Bambino for 31,458 days. That is the number of days from their 1918 World Series Championship to their 2004 Game 4 victory over the St. Louis Cardinals. It took them only 1,096 days to win their seventh World Series title in 2007.

Jonathan Papelbon is only the seventh Red Sox player to wear jersey No. 58. This number was not used by any player or coach until 1993. Jeff McNeely was the first player to don the number. Bill Moloney later became the first staff member to wear it in 1997.

Red Sox legend Jim Rice had 58 career stolen bases to his credit. Rice's Hall of Fame career in Boston was played from 1974-89. He was also an eight-time All-Star selection during those years.

Since 1972, the Red Sox individual record for the most game-tying and go-ahead RBIs is 58, which was set by none other than Jim Rice. Rice had 58 GT/GA RBIs in 1978.

In 1985, Wade Boggs set a single-season club record in the category of the most plate appearances by a Red Sox. Boggs set the record with 758 plate appearances that season.

From 1951-59, Sammy White recorded 4,458 career putouts for the Boston Red Sox. This ranks him 4th on the BoSox career list for the category.

By The Numbers

•••○○○

Boston Red Sox

○ ○ ○ • • • ⊕ 59

B
A
S
E
B
A
L
L

In 1959, the Red Sox became the last MLB team to integrate. Elijah Jerry "Pumpsie" Green became Boston's first-ever black player 12 years after Jackie Robinson debuted for the Brooklyn Dodgers.

Carl Yastrzemski had a total of 59 triples in his major league career. Yaz spent his entire 23-year career with the Boston Red Sox. His 59 triples place him 14th on the Red Sox all-time career list for the category.

The 1961 Boston Red Sox set a club record for the most one-run games. The team went 32-27 in 59 total one-run games played that year.

The most runs batted in by a left-hander in a single-season in Red Sox history are 159. This is another of the club's individual records held by the prodigious Ted Williams. "The Splendid Splinter" set this mark in 1949.

The Red Sox team pitching record for the most strikeouts in a single season is 1,259. Boston's pitching staff set this club record in 161 games played in 2001.

Wade Boggs had a career fielding percentage of .959. He is ranked 4th of all time on Boston's career fielding records list for third basemen.

The 2nd most career putouts by a Red Sox outfielder are 4,159. This was Ted Williams' total through his 19 seasons in Boston from 1939-42 and 1946-60.

By The Numbers

Boston Red Sox

BASEBALL

The earliest the Red Sox have achieved 60 wins in a season is July 16 (1978). The latest the club has achieved 60 wins is Sept. 29 (1923).

Boston's club record for the most total bases in a single game is 60. The record was set on June 8, 1950, versus the St. Louis Browns. This mark is a Major League Baseball record.

Red Sox player Bill Monbouquette set a club record for the longest errorless streak in consecutive chances by a starting pitcher from Sept. 9, 1962 to July 4, 1965. Monbouquette had 160 consecutive chances without an error during that span.

In 1902, Cy Young accounted for 160 strikeouts. He led all Red Sox pitchers with the most strikeouts that season. Young pitched 384.2 innings and had an ERA of 2.15 in 1902.

Harry Hooper set a Red Sox career fielding record for the most assists by an outfielder. From 1909-20, Hooper tallied 260 total assists.

Another of David Ortiz's career postseason records is for the most plate appearances. Ortiz has 260 postseason plate appearances in his career with the Red Sox.

Vern Stephens is ranked 8th of all time on the Red Sox career list for the most consecutive games played. Stephens played 360 straight games from April 19, 1948 through Aug. 28, 1950.

By The Numbers

Boston Red Sox

61

BASEBALL

What will 61 RBIs, 22 home runs and a .293 batting average get you? If you happen to be Carlton Fisk, and the year is 1972, it will get you the unanimous American League Rookie of the Year Award.

Carlton Fisk ended his Hall-of-Fame career with the Red Sox with 61 stolen bases to his credit.

In a remarkable coincidence, Carlton "Pudge" Fisk ranks 5th of all time on the Red Sox career list for the most double plays by a catcher with 61. Perhaps Fisk should have worn jersey No. 61.

Not many sports franchises are fortunate enough to replace one legend with another. Following 18-time All-Star Ted Williams' final game in 1960, who could have predicted that he would be replaced by an eventual 19-time All-Star? That is precisely what happened. Carl Yastrzemski's 1-for-5 performance in his first outing as a Red Sox on April 11, 1961, belied the stellar career he was about to have.

The second All-Star Game of 1961, which was played at Fenway Park, was the first-ever All-Star Game to end in a tie, 1-1. The game was called after the ninth inning due to rain.

Johnny Pesky had 361 total RBIs while playing for Boston. "Mr. Red Sox" played for Boston in 1942 and again from 1946-52.

By The Numbers

Boston Red Sox

○○○••• ⊕ 62

B
A
S
E
B
A
L
L

Fenway Park's press room was destroyed by fire on March 25, 1962. Thankfully it was not as devastating as the five-alarm fire that ravaged Fenway on Jan. 5, 1934.

The Red Sox scored 62 total points in ninth innings in 2010. This compares to 69 total points scored in the inning by their opponents.

Lou Criger, the first-ever Opening Day catcher, for the Red Sox (Boston Americans, 1901), ended his career in Boston with 62 double plays. He is ranked 4th on the all-time career list in the category.

Carlton Fisk finished his career with the Red Sox with 162 home runs. Pudge played for the BoSox in 1969 and again from 1971-80. Fisk did not play for Boston in 1970 due to military commitments and a stint in the minors.

Tris speaker is credited with 2,562 career putouts. He is ranked 7th of all time in the category for the most career putouts by a Red Sox outfielder.

One of nine Red Sox Hall of Fame Moments is Earl Wilson's no-hitter thrown on June 26, 1962, at Fenway Park. Boston defeated the Los Angeles Angels 2-0 that day, and Wilson became the first-ever black player in American League history to throw a no-hitter. The victory tasted even sweeter when he hit a home run that day.

By The Numbers

Boston Red Sox

○ ○ ○ • • • ───────────────── 63

B Sixty-three hits allowed is Boston's career
A postseason record for the category. Pedro
    Martinez is the current holder of that record.

S Fred Parent was part of the 1901 Boston American's
E roster. Parent hit 63 triples in his career, which ranks
B him 11th of all time on the Red Sox career leaders list
    for the category. At the time of Parent's death, he was
A the last surviving member of Boston's 1903 World
L Series Championship team.
L
    The Red Sox career postseason record for the most
    games played is 63, and it is held by current team
    captain Jason Varitek. He played his first postseason
    game for the Red Sox in 1998 and his most recent in
    2008.

The most games the Red Sox have ever played in a single season are 163. This has happened three times: 1961, 1978 and 1985. In the 1978 season, Jim Rice played every one of the 163 games. In doing so, he set a record for the most games played by a Red Sox in a single season.

In 2005, David Ortiz broke into the top 10 in the category of most total bases by a Red Sox in a single season. Ortiz's 363 total bases that season earned him the No. 9 spot on the list.

Hobe Ferris had 3,063 career assists from 1901-07. He holds down the No. 2 spot on the Red Sox career list for the most assists by a second baseman.

By The Numbers

• • • ○ ○ ○

Boston Red Sox

○ ○ ○ ● ● ● 　　　　　　　　　　　　64

B
A
S
E
B
A
L
L

The Red Sox club record for the most sacrifice flies in a single season is 64. The 2003 team set this record in 162 games played.

Tris Speaker is credited with 64 double plays in his career in Boston. This ranks Speaker No. 1 for outfielders with the most double plays in team history.

On June 8, 1950, Red Sox batters faced the St. Louis Browns' pitcher 64 times. This set a team record for the most times faced pitcher in a nine-inning game.

The No. 8 spot on the Red Sox career fielding leaders list for the most games played by an outfielder is occupied by Mike Greenwell. Greenwell patrolled the outfield for the Red Sox from 1985-96. During those years, he played in 1,164 games.

The 1964 Boston Red Sox had two players on its roster who were, or would become, part of a duo of relatives who played for the team. Tony Conigliaro's brother, Billy Conigliaro, would join the team five seasons later. Ed. Connolly, Jr.'s father, Ed Connolly, Sr. had played for the Red Sox from 1929-32.

In 1986's American League Championship Series the Red Sox played in front of 64 thousand-plus in three consecutive games at the California Angels. The games are ranked first through third for the largest road attendance for the Red Sox in the postseason.

By The Numbers

● ● ● ○ ○ ○

Boston Red Sox

BASEBALL

Third baseman Jimmy Collins in ranked 10th on the Red Sox all-time career list for the most triples. Collins had 65 triples from 1901-07.

In 1977 the Red Sox set a team best for the fewest games to reach 100 home runs. The 1977 team took only 65 games to reach the century mark that season.

The Red Sox record for the most runs in four consecutive games is 65. The record was set from June 5-8, 1950, versus the Chicago White Sox (June 5-6) and St. Louis Browns (June 7-8). The respective scores for those four games were: 12-0, 4-8, 20-4 and 29-4.

Johnny Pesky hit 165 singles his rookie season, 1942. He set the single-season rookie record for the category that year.

The Red Sox rookie record for the most total bases in a season is 365. Nomar Garciaparra set the mark in 1997.

Wade Boggs recorded the 2nd most career putouts by a Red Sox third baseman. Boggs' 1,165 putouts were recorded from 1982-92.

On Sept. 16, 1965, right-handed pitcher Dave Morehead no-hit the Cleveland Indians at Fenway Park. In nine innings pitched, Morehead walked one batter and struck out eight others. The Red Sox handed the Indians a 2-0 loss that day.

By The Numbers

Boston Red Sox

○○○ • • • ────────────── 66

BASEBALL

Ted Williams earned the No. 5 spot on the Red Sox single-season list for the most multi-hit games with 66 in 1940.

Hideki Okajima's Red Sox rookie record for the most games played was set in 2007. Okajima played 66 games that record-setting season.

The fewest errors Boston has ever committed in a single season are 66. In 162 games played in 2006, Red Sox fielders mishandled the remarkably low number of balls.

In his career Dick Gernert hit 66 home runs at Fenway. This achievement places him in the top 25 of all Red Sox batters. Gernert holds the 22nd overall spot on the career list for the most home runs at Fenway.

One hundred sixty-six days spent in first place in 2007 is a record for the Red Sox. Boston has never enjoyed more consecutive days in first place in its team history.

The only Red Sox player to ever wear jersey No. 66 was Joe Cascarella in 1935. Cascarella switched to jersey No. 19 for the 1936 season, his last season as a Red Sox.

Right-handed pitcher George Winter is ranked 2nd of all time on the Red Sox career leaders list for the most assists by a pitcher. Winter tallied 466 assists from 1901-08.

By The Numbers

Boston Red Sox

BASEBALL

The MLB and Red Sox record for the most doubles hit by a player in a single season is 67. Earl Webb set the record in 1931. Due to the nature of modern ballparks, this record is not likely to be broken.

Pedro Martinez set a Red Sox pitching record in 2000 for the lowest opponents batting average, which was a resoundingly low .167 batting average. Not surprisingly, he also set and currently owns MLB's record for the category as well.

In 1925, Ted Wingfield set a Red Sox record that is probably every rookie pitcher's worst fear: the most hits in one year. Not a record a rookie pitcher wants to be associated with, Wingfield allowed 267 hits over the course of the 1925 season.

Seven-time All-Star and Hall of Famer Joe Cronin recorded 1,767 career putouts from 1935-45. Cronin earned himself the No. 5 spot on the Red Sox career fielding leaders list for the most putouts by a shortstop in the process.

1967 was the year of the "Impossible Dream" pennant. On the heels of 1966's losing campaign, Boston had much to prove. The 1967 race for the pennant came down to the last day of the regular season. In the end, Boston's 92-70 record was just enough to edge out the Detroit Tigers and Minnesota Twins to win the American League pennant by a single game.

By The Numbers

Boston Red Sox

BASEBALL

Wade Boggs and Nomar Garciaparra have both had 68 multi-hit games in a single season for the Red Sox, and both led the league the year they did it. Boggs did this in 1983 and Garciaparra followed in 1997. Their 68 multi-hit games rank them 3rd on Boston's all-time list for the category.

Bill Lee accumulated 68 losses during his pitching career in Boston. Lee called Boston home from 1969-78. His 68 losses place him at No. 20 on the Red Sox career list.

Frank Malzone hit 68 career home runs at Fenway Park. Malzone's hits came during the 1955-65 seasons. Only 20 other Red Sox batters have hit more at Fenway in their careers.

Take a look at the Red Sox career pitching leaders' list for 10-strikeout games, and you will find Roger Clemens sitting in the No. 2 spot. Clemens enjoyed 68 10-strikeout games while playing in Boston.

Tom Gordon is credited with 68 career saves during his years in Boston. Flash is ranked 8th on the Red Sox career list for the category.

The No. 4 position on the Red Sox career fielding leaders list for the most putouts by a third baseman is filled by Jimmy Collins. From 1901-07, Collins recorded 968 putouts to earn his spot on the list.

By The Numbers

Boston Red Sox

○○○••• ──────────────── 69

B
A
S
E
B
A
L
L

In 1998, Tom Gordon finished 69 games, and in doing so he set a Red Sox pitching record for the most games finished in a single season.

Fred Lynn holds the No. 20 ranking for the most career home runs at Fenway Park. Throughout his career in Boston Lynn hit 69 home runs to earn his position on the leaders list.

Jim Rice is ranked 2nd of all time for the most multi-hit games by a Red Sox batter in a single season. Rice had 69 multi-hit games in 1978. He also led the league in the category that year.

The Red Sox career postseason record for the highest batting average was set by Carl Yastrzemski. Yaz was 24 for 65 in postseason play in 1967 and 1975, for a .369 batting average.

Nomar Garciaparra finished his Red Sox career with a .969 fielding percentage. He occupies the No. 5 spot on the Red Sox career list for the highest fielding percentage by a shortstop.

Featured Figure

In 1969, Red Sox fans voted for their All-Time Team. That year's vote resulted in the following selections: C Birdie Tebbetts, 1B Jimmie Foxx, 2B Bobby Doerr, 3B Frank Malzone, SS Joe Cronin, OF Ted Williams, OF Carl Yastrzemski, OF Tris Speaker, RHP Cy Young and LHP Lefty Grove. Ted Williams was voted Greatest Player.

By The Numbers

•••○○○

Boston Red Sox

B A S E B A L L

In 1946, Boston won its 70th game on July 30. That is the earliest the team has ever won its 70th game. In 1905, 1920 and 1992, Boston won its 70th game on Sept. 27, which is the latest the team has ever won its 70th game.

Jacoby Ellsbury holds the Red Sox record for the most stolen bases in a single season. Ellsbury stole 70 bases in 2009. He led the league that season as well.

Seventy home runs hit at Fenway is Vern Stephens' career total. He sits in the 19th spot for the most career home runs at Fenway. Stephens played for Boston from 1948-52.

Joe Cronin ended his Red Sox career with 270 doubles to his name. He ended his MLB career with 170 home runs. Cronin played for the Red Sox from 1935-45. Prior to playing for Boston, he played for the Pittsburgh Pirates from 1926-27 and the Washington Senators from 1928-34.

Jim Rice took 670 bases on balls in his career. Rice spent his entire career in Boston. He was an instrumental member of BoSox rosters from 1974-89.

With 1,370 career putouts, Jerry Remy is ranked 6th of all time on the Red Sox career fielding leaders list for the most putouts by a second baseman. Remy joined the Red Sox in 1978 and played with the team through the 1984 season.

By The Numbers

Boston Red Sox

71

BASEBALL

Doc Cramer holds the Red Sox record for the most at-bats without a home run in a season. However, Cramer's 658 at-bats in 1938 did result in 71 RBIs and a .301 batting average.

Holding down the No. 9 spot for the most career triples by a Red Sox batter is Ted Williams. The Splendid Splinter hit 71 triples among his many other accomplishments in Boston.

The fewest double plays the Red Sox have ever had in a single season are 71. The 1908 team turned the 71 double plays in 155 games.

Dennis Eckersley tallied 71 losses in his career in Boston. He is ranked 19th for the most losses in a career.

With 71 career double plays, Jason Varitek sits in the No. 2 spot for the most double plays by a catcher in Red Sox history.

Jersey No. 71 has never been issued by the Boston Red Sox organization.

Vern Stephens played for the Red Sox from 1948-52. During his career in Boston, he recorded a .971 fielding percentage. He is ranked 2nd of all time on the career fielding leaders list for the highest fielding percentage by a shortstop.

By The Numbers

Boston Red Sox

BASEBALL

In 1985, Wade Boggs established the Red Sox current record for the most multi-hit games in a season. That year Boggs had 72 multi-hit games.

Hall of Famer Rickey Henderson played exactly 72 games for the Boston Red Sox in 2002. Henderson was inducted into the National Baseball Hall of Fame in 2002.

Boston's career pitching record for the most 10-strikeout games is 72. It is held by Pedro Martinez and was set from 1998-2004.

The highest career fielding percentage ever achieved by a Red Sox third baseman is .972. The mark was set by Mike Lowell from 2006-10.

Derek Lowe's career fielding percentage in Boston was .972. It was good enough to earn him the No. 8 position on the Red Sox career leader board for the highest career fielding percentage by a pitcher.

Carlton Fisk was unanimously voted the 1972 American League Rookie of the Year. Pudge played in 131 games that season. His stats that year include 134 hits, 28 doubles, nine triples, 22 home runs and a .293 batting average.

Second baseman Doug Griffin and catcher Carlton Fisk were awarded with Rawlings Gold Glove Awards in 1972. It was the first and only year either of the two players would win the award.

By The Numbers

Boston Red Sox

○○○••• ────────────── 73

BASEBALL

Red Ruffing is ranked 20th overall for the most complete games pitched by a Red Sox pitcher. Ruffing pitched 73 complete games from 1924-30.

Ranked No. 15 on the Red Sox career leaders for the most losses is Bruce Hurst. From 1980-88 Hurst accumulated 73 losses. He finished his career in Boston with an 88-73 record.

From June 23 to Sept. 19 (G2), 1948, Bobby Doerr enjoyed 73 consecutive errorless games. His streak is the longest in a single season by a Red Sox second baseman.

J. "Shano" Collins ended his managerial career in Boston with a 73-134 overall record, for a .353 winning percentage. Collins spent 1931-32 as Boston's skipper.

Jim Rice amassed 373 doubles during his Red Sox career. The record was good enough to earn him the No. 6 spot on the career list for the category.

Daniel Bard (2010), Manny Delcarmen (2008) and Tom Gordon (1998) have all pitched 73 games in a season. They are among the leaders for the most games pitched in a single season by a Red Sox pitcher.

From 1940-42 and 1946-53, Dom DiMaggio played in 1,373 career games for the Red Sox. It was enough games to earn him the No. 6 spot on Boston's career fielding leaders list for the most games played by an outfielder.

By The Numbers

────────────── •••○○○

Boston Red Sox

BASEBALL

Rob Murphy owns the Red Sox single-season record for the most games pitched by a left-handed pitcher. He set the mark with 74 games in 1989.

In 1999 and 2000, Derek Lowe pitched in 74 games for the Red Sox. Lowe had a career-low 2.56 ERA in 2000 and a comparable 2.63 ERA in 1999.

Sitting in the No. 18 position for the most home runs hit at Fenway Park in a career is Joe Cronin. Cronin spent the 1935-45 seasons sending baseballs over Fenway's walls. During those seasons he hit 74 home runs at home.

The most double plays Red Sox batters have ever grounded into in a season are 174. In 1990, Boston grounded into 174 double plays in 162 games played. They set an MLB record for the category that season.

Boston's club record for the most RBIs in a single season is 974. Red Sox batters hit the record-setting total in 154 games in 1950.

Featured Figure

Seventy-four thousand-plus fans crowded into Yankee Stadium on May 26, 1947, to watch the Red Sox-Yankee rivalry game. Verified attendance was 74,747, which is the second highest all-time attendance for a Red Sox road game. The Yankees won the game 9-3 that day.

By The Numbers

Boston Red Sox

○○○•••

BASEBALL

Mel Parnell played for the Red Sox from 1947-56. During that time he lost 75 decisions. He ended his career with a 123-75 record, a 3.50 ERA and 732 strikeouts. His 75 losses rank him No. 14 on the career list for the most losses.

In 1996, Heath Slocumb played in 75 games. He is currently ranked 5th for the most games played by a Red Sox pitcher in a single season. Slocumb finished the 1996 season with a 5-5 record, a 3.02 ERA and 31 saves.

Jerry Remy is ranked ninth on Boston's single-season list for the most at-bats without a home run. Remy's 592 at-bats led to 43 RBIs and an average of .275 in 1983. Unfortunately though, he did not have a single home run.

Boston's single-season record for the most RBIs by a right-hander is 175. Jimmie Foxx set the record in 1938. Foxx earned the American League Most Valuable Player Award that year thanks to his league-leading RBIs, 50 home runs and .349 batting average.

Featured Figure

The all-time highest attendance recorded at a Red Sox road game is 75,997. The attendance was tabulated at a game held in Cleveland, Ohio on Aug. 26, 1951. The Cleveland Indians stole a 2-1 victory from the Red Sox in front of the record crowd.

By The Numbers

Boston Red Sox

○○○●●●

BASEBALL

In 1918-19 Everett Scott had a single-season fielding percentage of .976. He holds the No. 8 and No. 9 spots on the Red Sox single-season leaders list for the highest fielding percentage by a shortstop.

Seventy-six home runs earn Reggie Smith the No. 17 ranking on Boston's list of career home run leaders at Fenway Park. Smith hit his home runs from 1966-73 before moving on to the St. Louis Cardinals.

Thanks to a 76-game errorless streak from April 4 to Oct. 2, 2004, Mike Timlin has a firm grip on the Red Sox single-season record for the most consecutive games without an error by a reliever.

Reggie Smith owns the Red Sox record for the most hits by a switch hitter in a single season. His record 176 hits led to 109 runs, 32 doubles, seven triples, 22 home runs and a .309 batting average that season.

Johnny Pesky scored 776 runs during his 8-year career in Boston. The runs resulted from 4,085 at-bats. He is ranked 9th on Boston's career leaders list for the most runs.

Tom A. Yawkey died on July 9, 1976. His wife, Jean R. Yawkey, became the club's president following his death. That same year, the City of Boston changed the name of Jersey Street to Yawkey Way in his honor. To this day, Red Sox fans can still read TAY and JRY written in Morse code on Fenway's manual scoreboard in remembrance of the longtime owners.

By The Numbers

Boston Red Sox

○ ○ ○ ● ● ● — 77

B
A
S
E
B
A
L
L

Right-handed pitcher Willard Nixon played for the Red Sox from 1950-58. During his career in Boston he recorded a .977 fielding percentage. He earned a top-five ranking for the highest career fielding percentage by a pitcher with that average.

Joe Foy suited up for the Red Sox from 1966-68. During that time he participated in 77 double plays. He's ranked 10th for the most double plays by a third baseman in team history.

Seventy-seven Red Sox were hit by pitch in 1909. In addition to bruised bodies and egos, the hits by pitch left a mark on Boston's record books. To this day, it remains the greatest number of times Red Sox batters have been hit by pitch in a single season.

Rico Petrocelli's 77-game errorless streak in 1971 qualifies for both the most consecutive games without an error in a season and in the career of a Red Sox third baseman.

From 1901-07 Hobe Ferris hit 77 triples. It was enough to earn him the No. 7 spot on the Red Sox list for the most triples.

The 177 home runs that Nomar Garciaparra hit during his years in Boston are the most ever by a Red Sox shortstop. Ted Williams' 477 home runs are the most by any Red Sox left fielder.

By The Numbers

Boston Red Sox

BASEBALL

Since the new Red Sox ownership group took control of the team in 2002, Boston has a .578 winning percentage. The team has an 842-616 record since the change.

From 1926-32 Danny MacFayden was a Red Sox pitcher. MacFayden was eventually traded to the New York Yankees, but not before going 52-78 from the mound for the Red Sox.

Pudge Fisk played in 1,078 games from 1971-80. In his 11 seasons as a Red Sox he had 4,353 plate appearances, 3,860 at-bats, 1,097 hits and scored 627 runs.

Second baseman Marty Barrett joined the Boston Red Sox in 1982. Through 1990, Barrett had recorded 578 career double plays. He is ranked 2nd of all time behind Bobby Doerr in the category.

Outfielders Dwight Evans and Fred Lynn won Gold Glove Awards in 1978. Lynn won a total of four Gold Gloves in his career, and Evans won eight.

Jim Rice was named the 1978 American League Most Valuable Player. That season, he also won the RBI and home run crowns.

In 1978, a partnership made up of Jean Yawkey, Haywood Sullivan and Edward "Buddy" LeRoux, Jr. purchased the Red Sox club from the Yawkey Estate. The American League approved the transaction on May 23, 1978.

By The Numbers

Boston Red Sox

BASEBALL

Jim Rice hit 79 triples during his 16 seasons with the Red Sox. It was good enough to earn him the No. 6 spot on Boston's career list for the most triples.

In 1964, Dick Radatz pitched in 79 games. He is currently ranked 3rd on the Red Sox list of single-season leaders for the category.

The most career double plays by a Red Sox catcher are 79. Sammy White set the record while playing for the BoSox from 1951-59, earning an All-Star selection in 1953.

In 1985, Marty Barrett had 479 assists. His performance earned him the No. 6 spot on the Red Sox single-season leaders list for the most assists by a second baseman.

1979 was a year of milestones for Carl Yastrzemski. On June 16, Yaz hit his 1,000th extra base hit, on July 24, he hit his 400th career home run and on Sept. 12, he collected the 3,000th hit of his career.

Left-handed pitcher Tom Burgmeier was named the BoSox Club Man of the Year in 1979. Thirty-five years old in 1979, Burgmeier enjoyed a 2.74 ERA and a .600 winning percentage that season. In 88.2 innings pitched Burgmeier allowed 89 hits, 32 runs, and eight home runs.

By The Numbers

Boston Red Sox

○○○••• ——————————————— 80

B
A
S
E
B
A
L
L

Boston's single-season record for the best stolen base percentage is 80.0. This record was matched two times in club history. The first time was in 2007 (96 SB/24 CS), and the second occurrence was in 2010 (68 SB/17 CS).

Pedro Martinez has 80 career postseason strikeouts. No other Red Sox pitcher has matched his record.

Jason Varitek's 80 career home runs at Fenway Park are good enough to place him 16th on the Red Sox list for the most home runs at Fenway.

On Aug. 16, 1946, the Red Sox won their 80th game of the season. It is the earliest date the team has ever won their 80th game. Excluding 2001, the team has never won their 80th game later than Oct. 1, which they did in 1937.

Dwight Evans played 380 consecutive games from Oct. 4, 1980 through Aug. 6, 1983 – the seventh longest consecutive game streak in Red Sox history.

Carlton Fisk had 480 assists during his career. He ranks 5th of all time for the most career assists by a Red Sox catcher.

RHP Chuck Rainey was named AL Pitcher of the Month for his play in May 1980. That same year, RHP Bob Stanley received the honor in the month of August. Later, Jim Rice completed the Red Sox hat trick by earning the Player of the Month Award in September.

By The Numbers

•••○○○

Boston Red Sox

B A S E B A L L

Mike Timlin pitched in 81 games in 2005. He had a 7-3 record and 2.24 ERA. His 81 games pitched are the most ever by a Red Sox pitcher, including the most by a right-handed pitcher, in a single season.

RHP Luis Tiant racked up 81 career losses from the hill during his eight-year career in Boston. This ranks him 11th of all time on the BoSox career leaders list.

From 1937-51 Bobby Doerr hit 381 doubles for the Red Sox. He is ranked 5th on Boston's all-time list for the most doubles hit in a career.

Boston's club record for the most at-bats in a single season is 5,781. The record was set in 162 games played in 1997.

In 1943 Lou Lucier wore jersey No. 81. Lucier played two seasons in Boston before moving on to the Philadelphia Phillies. During his short stint with the Red Sox (1943-44) he also wore jersey No. 15 and No. 24.

In 1981, Dwight Evans was awarded the Thomas A. Yawkey Red Sox Most Valuable Player Award. That same season, Jerry Remy was named BoSox Club Man of the Year.

Third baseman Carney Lansford and right-fielder Dwight Evans were presented American League Silver Slugger Awards in 1981. Evans also received a Rawlings Gold Glove that season.

By The Numbers

Boston Red Sox

BASEBALL

Since 1946, the fewest home runs the Red Sox have allowed in a season are 82. The current club record was set in 1949.

Jim Rice hit a total of 382 career home runs for the Red Sox. His home run total places him in 3rd place on Boston's all-time career home runs leaders list.

Boston's club season record for the fewest strikeouts is 282. Red Sox batters set this team record in 135 games played in 1901.

The single-season record for the highest winning percentage by a Red Sox pitcher is .882. The mark was set by Bob Stanley in 1978. That season Stanley had a record of 15-2.

Featured Figure

In 1982, for the second time in club history, fans were allowed to vote for their Red Sox All-Time Teams. The voting resulted in First Team selections of: C Carlton Fisk, 1B Jimmie Foxx, 2B Bobby Doerr, 3B Rico Petrocelli, SS Rick Burleson, OF Ted Williams, OF Carl Yastrzemski, OF Dwight Evans, RHP Cy Young, LHP Babe Ruth, REL Dick Radatz and MGR Dick Williams. Second Team selections were: C Birdie Tebbetts, 1B George Scott, 2B Jerry Remy, 3B Frank Malzone, SS Johnny Pesky, OF Jim Rice, OF Dom DiMaggio, OF Fred Lynn, RHP Luis Tiant, LHP Lefty Grove, REL Sparky Lyle and MGR Joe Cronin.

By The Numbers

Boston Red Sox

○ ○ ○ • • •

B
A
S
E
B
A
L
L

The Red Sox record for the highest single-season spring training batting average is .483. The record is held by Mo Vaughn who went 28-58 during spring traning in 1998.

Howard Ehmke and Sam Jones both pitched 83 career complete games for the Red Sox. Ehmke played for the Red Sox from 1923-26 and "Sad" Sam Jones from 1916-21. They are ranked 16th and 17th on Boston's career leaders list for the category.

In 2008, Dustin Pedroia had 83 RBIs, along with 17 home runs and a .326 batting average. The BBWAA presented him with the American League Most Valuable Player Award for his efforts.

Tris Speaker had a .383 batting average in 1912. He is ranked 3rd on Boston's single-season batting average list.

Dom DiMaggio and Fred Lynn both recorded a .383 career on-base percentage. DiMaggio is 15th and Lynn 16th on the Red Sox career list for the category.

From 1935-47 Joe Cronin amassed 1,883 total bases. That productivity has earned him the No. 19 spot on the Red Sox career leaders list for the most total bases in a career.

Wade Boggs earned an American League Silver Slugger Award in 1983. That season Boggs had 100 runs, 210 hits, 44 doubles, 7 triples, 5 home runs and a .361 batting average.

By The Numbers

• • • ○ ○ ○

Boston Red Sox

○○○•••

BASEBALL

Carlton Fisk ended his career with the Red Sox with a .284 batting average. Fisk had 3,860 at-bats and 1,097 hits in his 13 seasons in Boston.

The longest on-base streak in Red Sox history was set by Ted Williams in 1949. That season Williams set an MLB record by getting on-base in 84 straight games.

Johnny Pesky had 184 putouts in 1949. That performance earned him the No. 4 spot on Boston's single-season leaders list for the most putouts by a third baseman.

Bill Buckner holds Boston's single-season record for the most assists by a first baseman. Buckner set the team record in 1985 with 184 assists. He also led the league that season.

Nomar Garciaparra set Boston's single-season record for the most at-bats with 684 in 1997. Since it was his rookie season, it is also the team's rookie record for most at-bats in a single season.

During 19 seasons of play for the BoSox Ted Williams amassed 4,884 total bases. He is ranked 2nd on the Red Sox career list for the category.

The last originally-scheduled single-admission doubleheader in Red Sox history was on July 27, 1984. Boston traveled to Detroit for a four-game series, including the doubleheader on the 27th. The Red Sox and Tigers split the doubleheader 1-1.

By The Numbers

•••○○○

Boston Red Sox

BASEBALL

The BoSox record for the most career relief wins is 85. The record was set by Bob Stanley from 1977-89. Stanley spent his entire career in Boston, played in 637 games and finished 376 games.

Derek Lowe recorded 85 saves while pitching for the Red Sox. Lowe was on Boston's roster for eight seasons, 1997-2004. He had a 70-55 record and a 3.72 ERA.

David Ortiz (2006), Nomar Garciaparra (2002 and 1997) and Ted Williams (1949) each had 85 extra base hits in a single season while playing for the Red Sox.

From 1902-06 and part of 1907, Red Sox player Bill Dinneen had a symmetrical 85-85 record. He is No. 9 on Boston's career list for the most losses by a pitcher.

Joe Cronin took 585 bases on balls in his Red Sox career. Cronin began his career with the Pittsburgh Pirates (1926-27), spent time with the Washington Senators (1928-34) before landing with the Red Sox in 1935.

From 1991-98, official scorers tabulated 785 career double plays for Mo Vaughn. This places him in the No. 2 position for the most double plays by a Red Sox first baseman.

Red Sox great Johnny Pesky had 4,085 at-bats in his illustrious career. His at-bats led to 776 runs, 1,277 hits, 196, triples, and 13 home runs.

By The Numbers

Boston Red Sox

BASEBALL

The most extra-base hits Jim Rice (1978) and Ted Williams (1939) ever had in a season are 86. They are 6th and 7th respectively on Boston's single-season batting leaders' list for the category. William's 86 extra-base hits were in his rookie season, so it set the club's rookie record as well.

Nomar Garciaparra and Jackie Jensen each hit 86 home runs at Fenway Park. Garciaparra is ranked 14th and Jensen 13th on the Red Sox career list for home run leaders at Fenway Park.

Frank Malzone had 286 career double plays. He ranks 2nd of all time on the Red Sox career leaders list for the most double plays by a third baseman.

In 1986, Marty Barrett was named the BoSox Club Man of the Year. That season Barrett had 713 plate appearances, 625 at-bats, 94 runs, 179 hits, 39 doubles, 60 RBIs and a .286 batting average.

Roger Clemens (April and June), Wade Boggs (May), and Bruce Hurst (September) were each named American League Player/Pitcher of the Month in 1986.

Featured Figure

Two Red Sox Hall of Fame Most Memorable Moments took place in 1986. First, on April 29, Roger Clemens pitched MLB's first-ever 20-K game versus the Seattle Mariners at Fenway Park. Then on Oct. 12, in Game 5 of the American League Championship Series, Dave Henderson hit a 2-out, go-ahead home run in the 9th inning.

By The Numbers

Boston Red Sox

BASEBALL

Rick Ferrell had a career fielding percentage of .987. He ranks 4th of all time on the BoSox career list for the highest fielding percentage by a catcher.

From 1915-19 the Red Sox had a right-handed pitcher named Carl Mays who was known for his ability to throw complete games. He tossed a total of 87 of them for Boston. Two of them, in fact, were on the same day (Aug. 30, 1918). He is the only BoSox pitcher to ever throw two complete games on the same day.

Manny Ramirez had 87 extra-base hits in 2004. That output has placed him in the No. 5 spot on the BoSox leaders list for the most extra-base hits in a single season.

The most singles ever hit by a Red Sox batter in a season are 187. It was Wade Boggs who set that mark during the 1985 season. His total production that year included 240 hits, 42 of them doubles, three triples and eight home runs.

In August of 1987 Dwight Evans hit 31 RBIs in 27 games. Including Evans' outbreak, Red Sox batters have had 22 30-RBI months since 1970.

The Red Sox franchise experienced another ownership change in 1987. Edward 'Buddy" LeRoux, Jr. sold his general partnership shares to The Jean R. Yawkey trust. With that transaction, the trust owned two of three of the outstanding general partnership shares in the team.

By The Numbers

Boston Red Sox

BASEBALL

Through the 2010 season the highest jersey number ever worn by a Red Sox player, staff member, manager or coach is the No. 88. Coaches Jason LaRocque and Alex "Mani" Martinez are the only two men to ever wear the number.

The No. 5 spot on the Red Sox career pitching leaders list for the most saves is held by Jeff Reardon. From 1990-92 Reardon patrolled the hill for the Red Sox collecting 88 career saves. Throughout his entire career in MLB Reardon accounted for 367 saves.

In their careers on the mound, Dennis Eckersley and Bruce Hurst each had 88 wins. Eckersley was a Red Sox for eight seasons, and Hurst for nine.

Bobby Doerr had a career batting average of .288. Doerr had 7,093 at-bats and 2,042 hits in 1,865 games as a Red Sox.

Manny Ramirez sits in the No. 3 spot on the Red Sox career list for the highest slugging percentage (minimum 1,500 at-bats). ManRam's slugging percentage while in Boston was .588.

The most games played in a career by a Red Sox first baseman are 988. George Scott earned the top spot in the category while playing for Boston from 1966-71 and 1977-78.

Jerry Remy had 1,988 career assists. He is ranked 4th of all time on the Red Sox list for the most assists by a second baseman.

By The Numbers

Boston Red Sox

○○○••• ——————————————— 89

B
A
S
E
B
A
L
L

Eighty-nine triples from 1937-51, were hit by Red Sox Hall of Famer Bobby Doerr. Born in Los Angeles, Calif., Doerr spent his entire big league career in Boston.

Red Sox starters allowed 89 home runs in 2010. Starters accounted for 1,011.1 innings pitched, 980 hits, and an ERA of 4.17.

Johnny Pesky had 189 career strikeouts during his years with the Red Sox. Pesky had 4,760 plate appearances during his eight seasons in Boston. Pesky also spent time on the Detroit Tigers' and Washington Senators' rosters.

In 2010, Adrian Beltre had 189 hits. Beltre also had 589 at-bats and a .321 batting average in his only season with the Boston Red Sox.

Cy Young holds the BoSox record for the most career assists by a pitcher. Young recorded 689 assists from 1901-08.

The Red Sox club batting record for the most strikeouts in a single season is 1,189. Red Sox batters set this mark in 162 games played in 2004.

The last time a Red Sox player recorded an extra-inning grand slam was on May 19, 1989. Dwight Evans belted the homer at Oakland against former Red Sox RHP Dennis Eckersley. The grand slam was hit in the 10th inning and helped the BoSox secure a 7-4 victory.

•••○○○

By The Numbers

Boston Red Sox

○○○•••

90

B
A
S
E
B
A
L
L

The Red Sox set their mark for the earliest date to achieve 90 wins in a season on Aug. 30, 1946. Conversely the latest date they ever won their 90th game was on Oct. 3, 1904.

Carlton Fisk hit 90 career home runs at Fenway Park. George Scott also hit 90 at Fenway. They are ranked 11th and 12th respectively on the list of Red Sox career home run leaders at Fenway Park.

Birmingham, Ohio's Dutch Leonard and Hollywood, Calif.'s Frank Sullivan each tossed 90 career wins for Boston. Sullivan wore the famous red sox from 1953-60 and Leonard from 1913-18.

Ray Collins recorded 90 complete games in his seven seasons on the mound for the Red Sox. Collins played in Boston from 1909-15. He signed as a Free Agent with the Red Sox in 1909 and spent his entire career with them.

In 1987, Red Sox pitchers allowed 190 home runs. That is the most home runs ever allowed by a Red Sox pitching staff in a single season.

The fewest hits Red Sox batters have ever had in season are 990. That season, the BoSox played 126 games.

Heinie Wagner recorded 2,590 career assists during his playing days in Boston. He is ranked 6th of all time for the most assists by a BoSox shortstop.

By The Numbers

•••○○○

Boston Red Sox

BASEBALL

In 2004, David Ortiz earned the No. 2 spot on the Red Sox list for the most extra-base hits in a single season. Ortiz ended the season with 91 extra-base hits.

Right-handed pitcher Tom Brewer finished his career with the Red Sox in 1961. Through eight seasons in Boston he tallied 91 career wins. His overall record was 91-82, for a .526 winning percentage. He is ranked 14th on Boston's career pitching leaders' list for the most wins.

Bill Monbouquette played at Boston from 1958-65. During those seasons he accumulated 91 losses. His career record was 96-91 and he is ranked 8th on Boston's career losses list.

Ninety-one career saves is enough to earn Ellis Kinder the 4th spot on Boston's list of career leaders for saves. Kinder called Boston home from 1948-55. During his eight seasons in Boston he pitched 1,142.1 innings. He also had 8 career shutouts.

The Red Sox club record for the highest slugging percentage in a single season was set in 2003. Through the season's 162 games played, BoSox batters combined for a .491 slugging average. It was good enough to earn them an MLB record.

1991 was the first-ever season the Red Sox printed player names on the back of their road jerseys. To this day they still do not wear jerseys with names while at home.

By The Numbers

Boston Red Sox

BASEBALL

Jimmie Foxx sits atop the Red Sox single-season list for the most extra-base hits. In 1938, Foxx had 92 extra-base hits. It was a season in which he also led the league.

The most home runs in a season by Red Sox teammates are 92. The duo of David Ortiz and Manny Ramirez set the club record in 2005. Ortiz hit 47 and Ramirez hit 45.

Boston's club record for the lowest slugging percentage is .292. The record was set back in 1907, a 155-game season.

The best record the Red Sox have ever achieved in the month of September is 19-5, a .792 winning percentage. This club record was set in 1949.

Roger Clemens was named the BoSox Club Man of the Year and the Thomas A. Yawkey Red Sox Most Valuable Player in 1992. That season he was also named the American League Pitcher of the Month twice, in May and August.

Featured Figure

Joe Cronin had 3,892 at-bats in his career in Boston. A right-handed batter, Cronin hit .300 during 11 seasons with the Red Sox. For his entire MLB career, he had a .301 batting average. Cronin's jersey No. 4 was retired in 1984 by the Red Sox and he was inducted into the National Baseball Hall of Fame in 1956.

By The Numbers

Boston Red Sox

BASEBALL

Bobby Doerr had a fielding percentage of .993 in 1948. It is the second highest-ever by a Red Sox second baseman.

In 2010, the Red Sox scored a total of 93 runs in sixth innings. Coincidentally, Red Sox opponents scored a total of 93 runs in fifth innings.

Carlton Fisk won the AL Rookie of the Year Award in 1972. Among his accomplishments that season were a .293 batting average, 22 home runs and 61 RBIs.

The No. 2 spot on the Red Sox list for the most at-bats without a home run in a season is occupied by Tom Oliver. In 1930, Oliver, who was well known as a slap hitter, had 646 at-bats not resulting in a single home run. His batting average for the season was .293 and he had 46 RBIs.

Steve Lyons is one of three position players noted as having caught in a game for the Red Sox. Lyons was briefly behind the plate on Sept. 8, 1993, at the Chicago White Sox. He caught the last of the 8th inning of that game.

First baseman Mo Vaughn was named the BoSox Club Man of the Year in 1993. That season Vaughn played in 152 games, had 633 plate appearances, scored 86 runs and had a .297 batting average.

In 1993, The Jean R. Yawkey Trust purchased the third general partnership interest from Haywood C. Sullivan.

By The Numbers

Boston Red Sox

94

BASEBALL

The fewest number of Red Sox to ground into double plays in a single season is 94. Throughout the 152 big league games played in 1942, BoSox batters had 5,248 at-bats resulting in the 94 GDPs.

Bill Lee was a left-handed pitcher who patrolled the mound for the Red Sox from 1969-78. Lee had a career record of 94-68 in Boston, for a .580 winning percentage. Lee is ranked 13th on the Red Sox leaders list for the most career wins.

The majority of Ellis Kinder's career was spent with the Boston Red Sox. During those seasons, Kinder earned himself a top-20 ranking (currently ranked No. 19) for the most home runs allowed by a Red Sox pitcher. Kinder allowed 94 home runs in his eight years in Boston.

Hall of Famer Bobby Doerr scored 1,094 career runs. Doerr accumulated his runs from 1937-51.

In 1955, Billy Goodman had 599 at-bats with no home runs. He's ranked No. 8 on Boston's list for the most at-bats without a home run. During this stretch, Goodman's batting average was .294.

The Boston Writers Chapter of the Baseball Writers' Association of America has given awards to Red Sox players since 1990. In 1994, Roger Clemens was given their Red Sox Pitcher Award, Carlos Rodriguez their Red Sox Rookie Award and Joe Gildea their Good Guy Award.

By The Numbers

Boston Red Sox

○○○••• ───────────────── 95

BASEBALL

Ellis Burks accumulated 95 stolen bases from 1987-92 and 2004. Jackie Jensen gathered 95 from 1954-59 and 1961. They are ranked 16th and 17th respectively on Boston's list for the most stolen bases in a career.

In 1904 the Boston Americans won 95 games. Their end-of-season record was 95-59. This gives the 1904 team the 7th best winning percentage in club history, .617.

Kevin Youkilis, Norm Zauchin and Stuffy McInnis each have had a .995 fielding percentage once in their careers. Youkilis had his in 2006, Zauchin in 1955 (led the league) and McInnis in 1919. They are ranked in the top 10 for the highest single-season fielding percentage by a Red Sox first baseman.

Carl Yastrzemski had 195 career assists. He is ranked 3rd of all time for the most assists by a Red Sox outfielder.

Featured Figure

When the Red Sox Hall of Fame was established in 1995, the inaugural class included 16 inductees who had previously been enshrined in the National Baseball Hall of Fame. Those automatic inductees into the new Hall were: Eddie Collins, Jimmy Collins, Joe Cronin, Bobby Doerr, Rick Ferrell, Jimmie Foxx, Lefty Grove, Harry Hooper, Herb Pennock, Red Ruffing, Babe Ruth, Tris Speaker, Ted Williams, Carl Yastrzemski, Tom Yawkey and Cy Young.

By The Numbers

Boston Red Sox

○○○●●●

96

BASEBALL

The Red Sox won 96 games in both 1948 and 1949. Their overall record in 1948 was 96-59, for a .619 winning percentage. Their 96-58 record in 1949 was good enough for a .623 winning percentage.

Jeff Offerman holds the Red Sox single-season record for the most bases on balls by a switch-hitter. Offerman took 96 bases on balls in 1999 to set the club record.

Bill Monbouquette and Tex Hughson each had 96 career wins for the Red Sox. Monbouquette had a 96-91 career record for a .513 winning percentage. Hughson had a 96-54 career record for a .640 winning percentage.

In seven seasons with the Red Sox, Red Ruffing had a 39-96 overall record. Ruffing is ranked No. 6 for the most career losses by a Red Sox pitcher.

In 1914, Dutch Leonard had an ERA of .96 in 224.2 innings pitched. That is the best-ever ERA by a left-handed pitcher in Red Sox history.

Vern Stephens tallied 396 career double plays from 1948-52. He is ranked 7th of all time on the Red Sox career leaders list for the most double plays by a shortstop.

Mo Vaughn was named the American League Player of the Month in May 1996. It was the only time he would receive the award in his 12-year career.

By The Numbers

●●●○○○

Boston Red Sox

○○○••• ──────────── 97

B
A
S
E
B
A
L
L

The most home runs a Red Sox pitching staff has ever given up at home in a single season are 97. The home runs were allowed in 81 home games played in 1966.

Red Sox RHP Bob Stanley is credited with 97 career losses. RHP George Winter also had 97 career losses. They currently own the No. 4 and 5 spots on the Red Sox career list for the most losses.

Red Sox Hall of Famer, Pudge Fisk had 1,097 career hits from 1969, 1971-80. Fisk's hits came off 3,860 career at-bats.

Johnny Pesky recorded 1,097 career putouts. Pesky owns the No. 9 spot on the Red Sox career leaders list for the most putouts by a shortstop.

Roger Clemens won the American League Cy Young Award in 1987. Clemens ended the season with a 2.97 ERA. He was tied for the league lead with 20 wins, and had 256 strikeouts.

In 1946 and 1948, Ted Williams' on-base percentage was .497. He led the league each season. He also earned himself the No. 5 and 6 spots on the Red Sox single-season leaders list for the category.

A Silver Slugger Award was given to Nomar Garciaparra in 1997. He was the American League's shortstop recipient of the award that season.

By The Numbers

•••○○○

97

Boston Red Sox

○ ○ ○ • • •

B
A
S
E
B
A
L
L

The year Tris Speaker won his American League Most Valuable Player Award, 1912, he had 98 RBIs. At the time the award was called the Chalmers Award.

Second baseman Dustin Pedroia had an errorless streak of 98 consecutive games from July 30, 2009 to May 19, 2010. His streak is an all-time record for Red Sox second basemen.

The most runs batted in by a Red Sox leadoff hitter are 98. Nomar Garciaparra set the record in 1997, the same year that he was awarded the American League Rookie of the Year Award. Including his 98 RBIs, Garciaparra also had 30 home runs and a .306 batting average.

Jim Rice had a career batting average of .298. The Hall of Famer played for the Red Sox from 1974-89.

Coco Crisp is ranked 5th for the highest single-season fielding percentage by a Red Sox outfielder. In 2007, Crisp recorded a .998 fielding percentage.

With 698 career double plays to his credit, Rick Burleson holds the No. 1 ranking for the most career double plays by a Red Sox shortstop. Burleson also holds the No. 8 spot on the Red Sox single-season list for the most assists by a shortstop. In 1975, Burleson recorded 498 assists to earn his place on that list. Burleson spent 1974-80 in a Red Sox uniform.

By The Numbers

• • • ○ ○ ○

Boston Red Sox

B
A
S
E
B
A
L
L

Turning ninety-nine years old in April 2011, Fenway Park is the oldest ballpark in major league baseball. With no plans to rebuild any time soon, current management has just completed their 10-year renovation project and is preparing for the park's centennial celebration in 2012.

In 1999, Knuckleball specialist Tim Wakefield added his name to an unusual list in MLB history. The list includes those pitchers who have recorded four strikeouts in an inning. On Aug. 10, 1999, Wakefield struck out four Kansas City Royals in the ninth inning to add his name to the list of 22 AL pitchers who have accomplished the same rare feat.

Atop the Red Sox career leader list for the lowest ERA (minimum 1,000 innings pitched) you will find Smoky Joe Wood. In eight seasons with the BoSox, Wood pitched 1,416.0 innings, allowing 485 runs. Wood posted a 117-56 career record, earning a .676 winning percentage and a 1.99 ERA.

Wade Boggs leads all Red Sox third basemen for the most double plays in a career with 299. Boggs was a Red Sox from 1982-92.

The third All-Star Game to ever be played at Fenway was held on July 13, 1999. Red Sox pitcher Pedro Martinez started the game for the American League. Martinez won the All-Star Game MVP Award that day, helping the AL to defeat the NL 4-1.

Boston Red Sox

○ ○ ○ • • • **100**

BASEBALL

Dom DiMaggio had exactly 100 career stolen bases for the Red Sox. The Little Professor's career in Boston included two stretches, one from 1940-42 and another from 1946-53.

From 1984-96 Roger Clemens pitched 100 complete games for the BoSox. Clemens is ranked No. 9 on Boston's all-time list for the most career complete games.

The 1950, 1964 and 1984 Red Sox each hit 100 home runs at home. Their production gives them the No. 11, 10 and 9 respective rankings on the Red Sox list for the most team home runs at home in a single season.

The earliest date the Red Sox have ever earned their 100th victory was Sept. 21, 1946. The latest date the team ever earned a 100th victory was Oct 6, 1015. Of course, the BoSox have only had 100 or more victories three times, in 1912, 1915 and 1946.

Ted Williams hit 100 or more RBIs in a season nine times. Jim Rice accomplished that same feat eight times. David Ortiz has done it three times in his career. They are ranked 1st, 2nd and 3rd respectively on Boston's list for the most career 100-RBI seasons.

The Boston Americans won their 100th game on June 5, 1902. The game was played at Cleveland. Cy Young earned the win that day in a final score of 3-2.

By The Numbers

• • • ○ ○ ○

All information in this book is valid as of the end of the 2010 season.